TERENCE CONRAN ON
London

conran
OCTOPUS

ENDPAPERS: Satellite photograph of Greater London.

PAGE 2–3: London panorama with St Paul's Cathedral

PAGE 4–5: Greenwich Reach with the Thames Barrier in the background.

LEFT: Notting Hill Carnival reveller.

ABOVE RIGHT: Beatles fans leave their marks at London's most famous pedestrian crossing.

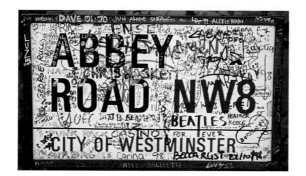

contents

Foreword

There can be little argument that London is one of the world's great cities. Along with New York, Tokyo, Paris, Rome and Berlin it can claim to be one of the most vibrant in the developed world – a wonderful and inspiring place to live and work. Like all such great conurbations, London is faced with the challenge of remaining a city where people not only visit, but want to stay and live. It is ironic that while cities have been the birthplace and driving force of so much of what we call 'civilisation', human beings have simultaneously struggled to civilise their own great cities. In this respect London is not unique.

Imperial Rome was the first city in human history to achieve a population of one million, and after its fall it was not until 1810 that London broke that record, reaching two and a half million by 1851, and eight million after the First World War. Now many cities around the world have surpassed London in terms of numbers. Across the third world new mega-cities see people living in conditions of poverty as bad as anything that existed in London in the nineteenth century. If we are lucky the

Terence Conran and Ken Livingstone at Bar Italia, phtographed for the Evening Standard, June 2000.

global population will stabilise at about nine billion by the middle of the twenty-first century. It is inevitable that the vast majority of people will live in great cities and if London, with all its wealth, cannot provide a decent quality of life for every citizen then what hope can there be for the inhabitants of Calcutta or Mexico City?

After decades of stagnation in the thinking of London's city managers and the closing down of the Greater London Council, London is now ripe for a period of major renewal. London has enormous advantages in the new economy; it contains Europe's financial centre; it leads Europe in the development of the internet, e-technologies and e-commerce; and it contains Europe's greatest accumulation of media industries.

London accounts for a sixth of the UK's production. No city in the world is more internationalised. As Terence Conran points out later in this book, London is a truly multi-racial city, where dozens of communities coexist – between a quarter and a third of London's population is non-white. If these strengths, which correspond perfectly to the new era we are entering, are properly harnessed, then London has the potential to become even more prosperous in the new economy than in the old.

As a boy growing up in London I felt safe to wander around and discover the city. It was many years before I was aware of the growth of sleeping rough or the steady increase in street crime. Buses were then still a universal mode of transport, rather than the creaking and unreliable 'integrated' service that we tolerate today.

Of course, London will not lose ground and will continue to build on its many strengths. However, I firmly believe that it is our collective task to ensure that London's undoubtedly exciting future is rooted in a sense of community, inclusivity and safety. Terence Conran, in producing this beautifully presented volume of his own observations of London, has made an important contribution to the need to constantly evaluate and re-examine our capital city. I hope that in enjoying this book, its readers will also use it to promote the idea that London must remain a place where the needs and aspirations of its citizens are central to the decisions that are made about its future.

Ken Livingstone *Mayor of London*

My London

Cities are all about change. More often than not, it is in cities that new trends tend to make their first appearance, that the cutting edge is sharpened and that experimentation throws up different ways of doing things. But some cities, at some times, change more than others.

As we enter the third millennium, London is poised on the brink of transformation. Everywhere you look, you see cranes. If the 'cranescape' is a good way of taking the economic pulse of a city, London is booming. It is estimated that by 2002 London will be the seventh-largest economy in Europe, surpassing Switzerland, Sweden, Finland and Hungary in gross domestic product. Yet while in economic terms London is a true city-state, I still like to think of it as a collection of eighty-odd villages loosely welded together.

London's cranescape is not just an indicator of prosperity and economic growth. The turn of the millennium has seen the fruition of many significant public projects – from Tate Modern at Bankside to the Millennium Bridge, from the London Eye to the Dome at Greenwich – which are set to alter permanently our perception and experience of the city. Rolled out on a wave of Lottery money – over 2 billion pounds worth – these new contemporary monuments collectively represent a radical redefinition of one of the world's favourite capitals. It is an exciting time to be a Londoner, and to be one of the city's many visitors.

The current redefinition of London is the latest development in a decade of tremendous change. London's traditions – its sense of history – have always been a huge draw for foreign visitors, but tourists today are equally attracted by the new restaurants and bars, hotels, galleries, clubs and shops that have sprung up in recent years. Bette Midler once said: 'If it's three o'clock in New York, it's 1938 in London.' Anyone coming to London today, expecting to see a city frozen in time, would have to put their watches forward quite a bit!

If I had written a book about London ten years ago, when I first had the idea, its contents would have been very different from what you are reading now. There are countless books about London, from tourist guides giving advice on eating and drinking, shopping and sightseeing in the city, to scholarly tomes detailing the capital's political and social evolution. I don't claim to be an historian, nor is my purpose here to provide a comprehensive listing of all the events and venues that London has to offer. What I promise instead is an unashamedly personal view of a city that constantly surprises, infuriates and inspires me.

Greenwich, looking across the Thames toward the bustling construction sites of east London. The Queen's House, designed by Inigo Jones, is in the foreground, with the National Maritime Museum behind. Beyond the museum, situated directly on the river, is the Royal Naval College, designed by Sir Christopher Wren, Nicholas Hawksmoor and Sir John Vanbrugh. Naval officers still trained there until fairly recently. After an abortive plan to sell the buildings, it was decided that they should form the permanent home of the University of Greenwich.

Dawn and dusk in the Square Mile, viewed through the clockface at the top of No. 1 Poultry, the James Stirling building where my restaurant Coq d'Argent is located. The neoclassical Royal Exchange is to the left, with the glinting steel ducts of Richard Rogers' Lloyd's Building behind.

I spent my early childhood in London, and I have lived and worked in London during my entire adult life. My father had a factory on the river at Stepney, importing and processing gum copal, the natural resin that was used in those prewar days to make paints and varnishes. I remember being taken as a child to visit the business, the pungent smell of the gum copal, and the bustling river traffic of what was then the world's largest port.

Like many London schoolchildren at that time, I made my first significant departure from the city with the outbreak of war. From urban leafy Hampstead my family decamped for what we imagined to be the comparative safety of Liphook in Hampshire, only to discover that our new home was directly below the flight path of German bombers, heading for the coast after their night-time raids and jettisoning their leftover bombs on an arms dump near our house. Later I was evacuated to stay with an aunt in Plymouth which, similarly, was perhaps not the wisest of moves. In any event, we managed to survive the war unscathed but our Hampstead house was completely destroyed.

My father's factory was another casualty of the war. Like much of the area around the docks, it was bombed to bits and, in the fire that followed, resin melted and flowed down the streets. Very little of the machinery or equipment was able to be salvaged afterwards. The safe was recovered intact, but encased in resin like a huge bar of toffee – or perhaps a proto-Rachel Whiteread.

After the war, London presented a scene of incredible devastation. Hardly a street seemed unmarked. It was this destruction of much of the city's fabric – a rupture that other great world cities such as Paris and New York do not share – that has contributed so much to London's present character. Yet, curiously, one of my strongest memories is not of the dereliction itself, but of the purple loosestrife, rosebay willowherb and buddleia that had quickly grown up to cover every bombsite. In a study carried out at the time by the Royal Botanic Gardens at Kew, 126 different species of flowering plants and ferns were recorded growing on London's bombsites, many of them never seen in the city before.

Rome is the 'Eternal City', Paris is the 'City of Light', but London is curiously undefinable. It is ancient and modern, progressive and stolid, grand and shoddy. The city's main newspaper, the *Evening Standard*, features a weekly questionnaire for London celebrities. 'If New York is the Big Apple, what is London?' is one of the regular questions. The answers, which tend to be fairly unconvincing variations on the fruit theme, reveal nothing so much as the difficulty of finding an image or phrase that encapsulates the glorious diversity of the city. Practically the only tag that has ever stuck is Samuel Johnson's 'Great Wen', but however littered the

The old and the new: conflicting faces of London's ever expanding Docklands redevelopment.

OVERLEAF: Images of 'red' London, a colour that evokes the authority, energy and traditions of the city.

streets or snarled the traffic, I cannot help but feel that London deserves better than to be compared to a boil. I rather prefer the image of a great octopus, with its tentacles drawing in cultural nourishment from around the globe …

There are so many different Londons, both real and imagined. Occasionally the imagined versions overlay the reality: it is hard to see certain areas of the East End as anything but Dickensian, while the upper-class enclaves of St James's seem lifted from the pages of an Evelyn Waugh novel. Tourists may search in vain for Sherlock Holmes on Baker Street and be similarly disappointed by the conspicuous absence of the London fog that swirls in the background of so many pre- and postwar films, but London literary locations are particularly alive in the imaginations of children. When Peter Pan flies off to Neverland with the Darling children, the nursery from which the children escape was modelled on a real Bloomsbury nursery, the night nursery of architect Sir Edwin Lutyens' children (he and the playwright J. M. Barrie were friends). Primrose Hill is identifiably the setting of the first link in the chain of the 'twilight barking' that culminates in the rescue of 101 Dalmatians. Children travelling through London's railway stations will undoubtedly keep an eye out for Paddington Bear, or the mysterious Platform nine and three quarters at King's Cross, from which the Hogwarts Express departs, taking Harry Potter and his friends to wizard school. From the 'Hampstead' novels of the chattering classes to the Soho of Colin MacInnes' *Absolute Beginners*, writers have added layers of meaning to the definition of the city.

The novelist and biographer Peter Ackroyd, one of the most acute interpreters of the city, defines London as 'masculine'. I was once talking to the head of Comité Colbert, a group formed to publicize the French luxury-goods business, who agreed with this. He pointed out that while French products such as perfume, *haute couture* and champagne have feminine associations, traditional British luxuries such as Savile Row suits, sporting equipment, whisky, tweed and leather are unashamedly male. London, as the trading capital where many of these goods are consumed, worn, used and marketed, does indeed have a masculine flavour, a quality reinforced by the sobriety of the architecture and the sense of security and stability that is generated by its role as a professional and financial centre.

More whimsically, Peter Ackroyd also characterized the city as 'red'. What a pleasing concept. Ceremonial, traditional London is conspicuously red: one has only to think of pillar boxes and old telephone boxes, the uniforms of Guardsmen and Yeomen Warders, double-decker buses and the Underground sign, flashes of official London red that emblazon tourist postcards – and of course our very first Mayor. But Ackroyd also

A traditional Catholic procession in Clerkenwell, an area that has long been home to many of the city's Italian immigrants.

associates London red with the conflagrations of the Great Fire and the Blitz, with violence, excitement and energy; with the vitality of the street – a quality that has increasingly expressed itself in London's creative industries in recent years.

Whatever gender or colour London may be, its most striking feature remains its lack of homogeneity. Today it is a truly multicultural city, where dozens of different communities coexist. A recent survey (published in *Multilingual Capital*, coedited by Dr Philip Baker and John Eversley) revealed that London schoolchildren speak 307 different languages and dialects, the greatest linguistic diversity in the world. After English, languages from the Indian subcontinent such as Bengali, Punjabi and Urdu are the most common, but Greek, Hebrew, Russian, Japanese, German, French, Spanish and Italian also feature in the top 40. For me, the fact that London is a cultural melting pot is one of its most attractive attributes.

London's diversity is also a product of its history, revealed in the patchwork of its architectural fabric. It is almost exactly 2,000 years old. Unlike other ancient cities, however, London is not stuck in a particular time frame. It is the product of constant reinvention. This dynamic of change has been driven by the fact that, ever since worldwide trading links were established in the reign of Elizabeth I, London has maintained its position at the forefront of cultural, financial and commercial developments. With the founding of the Royal Society and the Greenwich Observatory in the seventeenth century, London became a centre of intellectual pursuit and scientific enquiry and a place of international trade because of the invention of reliable methods of navigation. In the nineteenth century, it was an imperial capital; now its historical connections to ex-colonies in North America, the Asian subcontinent and the Far East, combined with its geographical position at the gateway to Europe, have earned it the status of a global city.

London has had no single Golden Age, spelled out in stone or bricks and mortar. Each period has left its mark. Roman London is still present in the straight lines of key thoroughfares running east to west and north to south; medieval London survives in the twisting alleys and lanes in the heart of the City and the odd, crooked half-timbered building. Neatly symmetrical Georgian squares coexist with grand Victorian terraces and modern high-rises. The hodgepodge of London's architectural styles reflects the many different roles it has played on the world's stage over time.

While much of London's ancient history lies buried, occasionally it surfaces in dramatic ways. In times past, buildings were torn down and thrown up in London with impunity, but nowadays a necessary preliminary of development in the city is the archaeological

ABOVE LEFT: Sikh leaders wash a flagpole with milk during the festival of Vasakhi.

BELOW LEFT: Chinese New Year celebrations in London's Chinatown.

investigation. A recent dig in Bishopsgate on the site of a proposed Norman Foster office block turned up a burial ground where some 8,000 medieval Londoners were interred. Their subterranean companion was an aristocratic Roman lady in a lead-lined sarcophagus; her reconstructed patrician features, the cosmetic tools and the richly embellished textiles buried with her, are now on display at the Museum of London. The fact that the remains of London citizens who lived nearly a millennium and a half apart were found in the same plot of land provides graphic evidence of London's layered composition, one slice of the past laid on top of another. I have to say, however, that most developers pray that nothing of interest lies under their sites. No. 1 Poultry, the City building designed by the late James Stirling and where my restaurant Coq d'Argent is located, was delayed by two years while the archaelogists carried out their dig, uncovering thousands of Roman artefacts.

London's architectural diversity is further proof of the haphazard nature of its development. With certain exceptions, London has generally resisted the grand design; it has never had a Baron Haussmann, or a modern urban supremo to organize its benevolent chaos. The result is that it has few grand vistas or thoroughfares, few

London provides a wealth of architectural and sculptural detail for dedicated 'lookers-up'. The entrance to Selfridges in Oxford Street is guarded by the 11-foot-high Amazonian figure of *The Queen of Time* by Gilbert Bayes (FAR LEFT). Broadcasting House, home of the BBC, in Portland Place, features sculptures by Eric Gill (LEFT). The figures over the main entrance are Prospero and Ariel (Ariel symbolizing the spirit of broadcasting). Gill worked on the sculptures in situ and the story goes that 'lookers-up' got more than they bargained for, as the eccentric artist wore flowing robes instead of trousers – but no underwear.

classical axes or vantage points and few really inspiring public places. Whenever the opportunity has arisen to impose an overarching design, events seem to have conspired to decide otherwise.

In 1666 Sir Christopher Wren planned a classical city to replace the areas of London lost to the Great Fire. After the six-day inferno, London was virtually a blank canvas. Seven-eighths of the City had been destroyed and, on the riverfront, hardly a single building was left standing from the Tower of London to the Temple. Wren presented his plan to Charles II barely a week after the fire had finally been extinguished. He had spent the previous eight months in Paris, and the avenues radiating from large circular piazzas, envisaged on his plan, displayed the same formal layout he had admired and studied in France. One feature of Wren's plan was a single quayside to unite the old Thames-side wharves in a single broad accessway, rather like a Paris boulevard. The basic concept was to eradicate the narrow winding streets of the medieval city, encouraging disease and decay – the 'Deformity and Inconvenience of the Old Town' in Wren's words – and replace them with a symmetrical street plan bisected by diagonal avenues connecting monuments such as St Paul's and the Royal Exchange with the new quayside and river.

Nelson looks down on Trafalgar
Square, site of countless rallies and
mass demonstrations, as well as
celebrations at Christmas and New
Year that are equally boisterous but
much less politically charged. The
so-called 'empty plinth' in the
north-west corner has been the
focus of much debate – it is as yet
undecided whom to commemorate
alongside Charles I and George IV,
so it will be filled with changing
pieces of contemporary sculpture.
A good idea, I think.

Visionary as it was, Wren's scheme was essentially impractical – not to mention ruinously expensive – and there is evidence that it was never even seriously considered. In characteristic and time-honoured fashion, the city was simply rebuilt along the previous (although in many cases widened) medieval streetlines – to proceed with a grand scheme such as Wren's, which took no account of existing property rights, would have entailed the payment of vast sums of compensation to landlords. This is not to say, however, that all opportunities for improvement were overlooked. London may have been rebuilt to a familiar street pattern, but it was rebuilt in brick and stone, not timber and thatch. A new domestic pattern – the 'rate houses' – was devised which gave the city a new quality of orderliness. The rate houses comprised three standard house designs, from two to four storeys, with specified wall thicknesses, detailing and locations: 'two storeys for bylanes, three storeys along the river and for streets and lanes of note, four storeys for high streets and mansion houses for citizens of extraordinary quality'.

The most ambitious replanning London has ever seen occurred not in response to disaster but rather out of a fortunate association between architect and royal patron in the early nineteenth century. For his client, the Prince Regent, John Nash conceived a classically inspired West End, which had a grand avenue, Regent Street, connecting the new Regent's Park, with its proposed ring of mansions and villas, with the Regent's palace in Pall Mall. Only eight of the villas Nash envisaged were actually built – a semicircle, not a ring – and much of Nash's Regent Street was rebuilt in the early twentieth century, but the clarity of the original scheme remains a defining feature of this part of central London. It was also Nash's idea to connect the seat of power at Westminster with the seat of commerce, the City, by means of an extended Pall Mall culminating in a new public square, Trafalgar Square.

A century and a half later, during the Second World War, the opportunity to replan a substantial part of the city arose again. Sir Edwin Lutyens was chairman of the planning committee set up by the Royal Academy to put forward new proposals for the rebuilding of London in the wake of the destruction caused by Hitler's bombers. The committee's ideas were published in 1942 as *London Replanned*. Like Wren, Lutyens foresaw great vistas from monuments such as St Paul's Cathedral to the river, broad open avenues and formal axes to provide an ordered coherence. Other ideas were concerned less with the appearance of the city and more with its workability. A proposal was included to link all main railway stations with a new underground line and ring road; another suggestion was to convert Covent Garden market into a centre for music and drama – an idea that was well ahead of its time.

Lutyens, like most of his fellow Academicians on the committee, was a classicist, favouring an architectural style that fell abruptly from fashion after the war when architects and planners became obsessed with the ideals of Le Corbusier and the Bauhaus. None of the ideas and recommendations featured in *London Replanned* were subsequently taken up. Neither were countless other plans in the postwar period that were concerned more with modernizing the infrastructure and improving the way traffic moved about the city. The idea of creating 'ring roads' – the term itself was new – to relieve congestion in the centre of London had been proposed as early as 1938 in the *Highway Development Survey for Greater London* prepared by Lutyens and Sir Charles Bressey. Sir Patrick Abercrombie's similar recommendations, put forward in his *Greater London Plan* of 1944, were also killed off by public apathy and lack of political will. Some might say that the unfortunate legacy of these missed opportunities remains with us today, in the chaotic and desperate state of London's transport system; others might be relieved that we were not afflicted with yet more roads. In any event, London rebuilt itself after the Blitz in piecemeal fashion, and often not very well.

The devastation of the Blitz and the often meretricious postwar development that succeeded it have incurred a predictable backlash in terms of planning, whereby the balance has tipped away from innovation in favour of conserving the past. This is understandable when so much of the city was lost in living memory, and so little of merit built to replace it. However, I believe that our current planning system has an unfortunate tendency to encourage mediocrity; the preservation of the past is sometimes achieved at the expense of frustrating what is new and potentially exciting. I very much doubt, for example, that the Michelin Building – resplendent with its outrageous and quirky advertising embellishments – which I bought and restored with Paul Hamlyn in the late 1980s, would receive planning permission today, yet it is now regarded as a landmark building of the early twentieth century.

I am all in favour of safeguarding what is truly fine in our architectural heritage, but excessive sensitivity to long-dead architectural styles has preserved much that is outdated and frankly unexceptional. Worse, perhaps (and this is a trend that defined much of the development of the 1980s), it has resulted in new buildings dressed up in fake Georgian and ersatz Victorian clothing, a 'style', accurately dubbed 'façadism', greatly in evidence in places such as Surrey Quays and other Docklands areas.

Great buildings do not arise from middle-of-the-road consensus or from focus-group deliberations; they are born out of risk, which inevitably means there is always the risk of getting it wrong. I believe that this is a risk worth taking; it's the price you pay for occasionally getting something truly great. On the whole, I would much rather see something – anything – happen than continue to witness the kind of stasis brought about by the endless ponderings of committees like the Royal Fine Arts Commission, which has tended to dumb down every exciting design to middle-of-the-road mediocrity.

In terms of development, one of the best things to happen to London in recent years was ironically the big property recession at the end of the 1980s – although it did not necessarily feel that way at the time. The effect of the recession was suddenly to release a great deal of property onto the market at substantially reduced prices, prompting new businesses to emerge from the economic downturn. Elsewhere, in Paris, for example, almost the reverse happened and, despite the recession, property remained tightly held by institutions that were determined not to let rental levels collapse.

Buildings do not last for ever, nor do they remain relevant; the pattern of life changes all the time. To my mind, the best type of conservation seeks to revive the old through innovation. It is what we have attempted to do in our development of the Great Eastern Hotel near Liverpool Street Station, a Grade II-listed Victorian railway hotel designed by Charles Barry, whose father (along with Augustus Pugin) was coarchitect of the Houses of Parliament. The building has many spectacular original features, not least of which is a glass-domed ceiling in what is now the restaurant Aurora; what we have been able to supply is two floors of new space, servicing and infrastructure that update the hotel for twenty-first-century use, and a strong but complementary design identity.

Creative transformation keeps a city alive and exciting. In London in recent years, redundant banks have become bars and restaurants, industrial warehouses have become loft apartments. This endless recycling of the city fabric provides both new ways of living and new business opportunities. In its way, it also serves to generate further vitality and diversity as different types of people rub up against each other and the creative sparks fly

Diversity gives texture, and texture in life is terribly important. A London that was perfectly ordered, litter-free, traffic-calmed, pedestrianized – as squeaky clean as modern Singapore, for example – would be a deadly dull place. It is the unexpected hidden nooks and crannies that make cities fascinating places to explore and London, thankfully, still provides an abundance of such moments – the city cherishes its privacy, its backwaters and secret places. The rather organic nature of London is undoubtedly part of its charm, and it says a lot about a persistent strain in the British character, an attitude that is suspicious of grand gestures and monuments and prides itself on 'muddling through'.

OVERLEAF: London's public buildings have made themselves over for the millennium, thanks to generous dollops of Lottery funding. In scope, ambition and sheer numbers of new projects, the changes have been breathtaking. LEFT TO RIGHT: Soane's Dulwich Picture Gallery has gained a new wing by Rick Mather; Jeremy Dixon and Ed Jones' reworking of the National Portrait Gallery features a new roof-level restaurant; and Somerset House, formerly a tax office, now houses the Gilbert Gallery, with its courtyard car park transformed into a stunning public venue.

London landmarks: The Monument, designed by Sir Christopher Wren, is the tallest standing stone column in the world and marks the place where the Great Fire began (ABOVE RIGHT). 'Justice' with her scales and sword stands atop the green dome of the Old Bailey, the Central Criminal Court where the country's most serious criminal cases have been tried since 1834 (ABOVE, FAR RIGHT). Perhaps London's best-loved statue, Eros wings his way over Piccadilly Circus, site of London's first illuminated advertisements (BELOW RIGHT).

OVERLEAF: The baroque splendour of St Paul's Cathedral by Sir Christopher Wren (LEFT) contrasts with the classical austerity of St Paul's Church, Covent Garden, by Inigo Jones (RIGHT). The Earl of Bedford, who commissioned the architect, stipulated that the church should neither be expensive nor any more elaborate than a barn. Inigo Jones replied that, in that case, the earl should have 'the handsomest barn in England'. The church has a long association with actors and the theatre.

At the same time, the downside of the 'muddle' is becoming increasingly apparent. In some areas of city life there is a fine line between happy disorder and outright breakdown. No one who has lived in London during the past decade could fail to notice the escalating pollution and the disintegration of the transport system, which can make the city so unpleasant on a daily basis. In terms of infrastructure, London simply does not work well. The scale of the problem is such that a solution will not be achieved in piecemeal fashion. If London is not to choke to death on fumes and traffic, an integrated transport policy for the capital is urgently needed. To adapt the New Labour soundbite from the last general election, the issues facing London today are: 'transportation, transportation, transportation'.

Astonishingly for a great world city, London only gained its first democratically elected Mayor in the year 2000. Ever since the Conservatives, and Lady Thatcher in particular, disbanded the GLC (Greater London Council), London has been without an official voice. For some, the new mayoral post offers the tantalizing potential of throwing up a Pasqual Maragall, the visionary Mayor of Barcelona, who almost single-handedly spurred the regeneration of the run-down inner-city harbour and put Barcelona on the international planning and design map. At the very least, it will prove an important means of establishing a platform for London issues to be aired and discussed. The new Mayor will undoubtedly need an appreciation of the different taste levels, both political and aesthetic, that naturally exist in a huge and diverse city.

And London is huge: a population of seven million and a gross area of 620 square miles. This immense scale is one of the aspects of the city that I find so inspiring. Every week I seem to discover something that I have never seen before. If London is hard to define, it is also dauntingly hard to know. Other cities, no matter how cosmopolitan, feel tiny by comparison.

That scale can be fully appreciated for the first time, in the breathtaking panorama provided by the new London Eye, the giant wheel audaciously sited directly opposite the Houses of Parliament. I'm glad to say I've been a supporter of the wheel ever since it was first proposed and I believe it will change people's view of the city for ever; literally so: on clear days, you can see for up to 25 miles in any direction. Equally important, the wheel serves to reorientate one's perception of the city at ground level, because you can see it from so many different places – by locating the wheel, you locate the Thames and gain a new understanding of how much the river loops and bends. Elegantly designed and engineered, higher than the Statue of Liberty, the wheel has seen off its critics by the sheer power of its optimism and delight. It is a fitting emblem for this new chapter in the life of London. Let us hope it becomes as symbolically important to Londoners as the Eiffel Tower is to Parisians.

London at Home

One of the persistent urban clichés that has attached itself to London is that it is a city of villages, and, as with all clichés, there is more than a little truth to it. What is now the vast sprawl of Greater London was indeed once a disparate collection of country hamlets scattered beyond the bounds of the walled city. In the seventeenth century, one of the diarist Samuel Pepys' favourite outings was a weekend jaunt to the village of Hackney to breathe the fresh air, admire the young women and sample the local strawberries – bucolic delights hard to imagine today in a borough that, for much of the past 100 years, has been a byword for urban deprivation. Few would disagree that there is equally little sign of the hare-coursing fields that gave Soho its name (after a hunting cry). Soho now has the highest density of population per square mile of any London area, swelled, on Friday nights, by more visitors per square mile than you would have believed possible.

Over the centuries London has inexorably encroached on these settlements and swallowed them up. London's first great property boom came with the Dissolution of the Monasteries in the sixteenth century, when the sudden availability of land previously held by the Church led to a soaring increase in inhabitants. In the eighteenth century the Georgians developed the areas to the west of the old city, laying out classical terraces, squares, circles and crescents from Bloomsbury to Belgravia. But the most dramatic change occurred between 1800 and 1914, when London's population rose sevenfold, and development spread outwards from the centre along the radial lines of the new railways. Unlike the high-rise cities of New York or Tokyo, where space is constricted, London has (until recently) largely grown outwards rather than upwards.

Today, little trace of London's original rural outposts remains. While some of London's prettier areas – such as Hampstead, Highgate, Barnes, Richmond and Kew – still have what approximates to countrified high streets, lined with small independent shops, pubs and local restaurants, nowadays the term 'village' is more likely to be employed by hopeful estate agents putting a gloss on fairly featureless suburbs.

In one sense, however, London is still a city of villages: it is profoundly territorial. Or perhaps it is more accurate to say it is a city of postcodes. These demarcations are more than they seem; they provide a way for Londoners to stake a personal claim on the overwhelming immensity of the city and in the process define their social status. There is a great deal of

In bed with the family, on the 18th floor of Trellick Tower, west London. The tower block, designed by Ernö Goldfinger, was once a notorious no-go area, with residents queuing up to leave. Now, after improvements, notably to security, the demand for flats is high and people are queuing up to live there.

PREVIOUS PAGES A few minutes past midnight, 1 January 2000. The Wheel was at a standstill due to a technical hitch and the long-awaited and much hyped 'River of Fire' did not quite materialize, but the millennium celebrations were nevertheless unforgettable.

snobbery – and inverted snobbery – involved in such distinctions, underscored by the urban lottery of property prices. Seasoned observers of the London landscape could probably predict how someone would dress, what they would read, what sort of car they would drive, what they would eat and drink, and probably even their children's names simply from knowing their postcode. Those who live in grey areas between boroughs both sought-after and somewhat less desirable inevitably reveal their tastes and aspirations when they describe their locations. A road referred to by the upwardly mobile as 'Islington fringes' may well be termed an unpoetic 'Dalston' by those who wear their street credibility with pride.

With the rise of property prices forcing middle-class families further from the centre, these distinctions become ever more fluid. When Chelsea became too expensive, for example, Fulham was suddenly socially acceptable. When Fulham came up in the world, Wandsworth was the next area to be colonized. When west London prices became prohibitive, the entrepreneurial and creative community turned its attention to east London, which is now fast becoming the chicest part of town. Such social and geographical nuances are beautifully observed in Henry Sutton's recent novel *The Househunter*, whose dissatisfied middle-aged heroine embarks on an obsessional London-wide search for a new house and thus a new life. She ventures further and further afield, trying on houses from Dulwich to Hackney to see if they will fit, but eventually comes full circle and changes her own house (and life) from within.

ABOVE: **Escalating house prices in London are making it difficult for many people to get a foot on the first rung of the property ladder.**

RIGHT: **The terrace pattern – Georgian, Victorian and Edwardian – defines much of London.**

As in any culturally diverse city, London's villages are also defined by the different nationalities that have created their own communities in the capital. Most people are aware of the fact that Australians and New Zealanders gravitate towards Earls Court and Shepherd's Bush, that Soho has its Chinatown, that there are large numbers of Irish living in Kilburn and that many people from the Caribbean have settled in Brixton. But there are other less obvious but equally distinct patterns: the Japanese in Finchley, Turks and Vietnamese in Hackney, Portuguese in Ladbroke Grove, South Africans in Hampstead and Ghanaians in Clapham. Such communities may not be quite so distinctive as Little Italy in New York, for example, but they add a vibrant dimension to the patchwork map of the city.

The big London divide has traditionally been north and south – north and south of the river, that is. Historically, the north bank of the Thames had a head start. The southern boundary of the medieval walled city was the river, while for centuries the other bank was the insalubrious and often marshy location of drinking dens, playhouses, brothels, pleasure gardens and the home of the lawless and dispossessed – just read Dickens to get the picture. Today, you can still encounter London cabbies who appear to believe it has not changed one jot.

But an equally distinct rift is between east and west, and, again, there are good historical reasons for it. With the prevailing wind from the west, the eastern areas of the city were literally 'downwind' of all the smoke from household fires and the stink of sewage and thus a natural site for polluting industry. The East End was also the point of disembarkation for immigrants in search of better lives or freedom from persecution, and many ventured no further than nearby streets. Only today, after the decline of the port of London and the departure of heavy manufacturing from the city, has a real opportunity arisen for the regeneration of east London. The gentle drift eastwards over the past 15 years has now become a headlong rush.

London may lack the sheer surging dynamism of Manhattan, the frenetic intensity of Tokyo or the elegant sophistication of European capitals such as Paris, but it remains one of the most liveable of the great world cities. At least part of that civilized quality derives from a certain stability of housing pattern: street after street laid out in Edwardian or Victorian terraces, or in Georgian garden squares. These earlier blueprints of design are often interspersed with high-rise tower blocks and newer, sometimes shoddier types of building but despite wartime bombing and some conspicuously unsuccessful postwar developments, London is a city where people can still feel at home. As visitors to the city constantly remark – and even some of its inhabitants are grudgingly prepared to admit – London is fundamentally a civilized place to live. Enthusiasts, myself included, would go as far as to say it is the best place in the world in which to live and work. I say this despite the fact that in recent years crime and the fear of crime has become an all too depressing aspect of living in London, with rates of burglary and car theft on the increase. You are much less likely to be murdered in London than in New York – or even Paris or Copenhagen – but the dismal frequency of break-ins means that many a London home, if not the proverbial Englishman's castle, is certainly fortified like one.

The survival of the terrace pattern has not been merely accidental – or just a bomber's or planner's oversight. From the heart of the city centre extending right out to the suburbs, these streets of low-rise houses, more often than not with garden space in front and to the rear, have proved a surprisingly flexible and accommodating framework for individual tastes and lifestyles. London's back gardens not only provide personal patches of countryside but are often hives of activity, with the ubiquitous garden shed serving as a setting for everything from seed propagation to boat-building, car maintenance to DIY.

Much of London's housing could be described as 'the same, but different'. Before the fashion for remodelling interiors took hold, one could enter the average terraced house and predict with some accuracy where the bathroom and kitchen would be. From the outside, there was equivalent uniformity. Some 70 years ago, for example, Vanessa Bell, sister of Virginia Woolf and one of the founders of the Bloomsbury Group, caused a considerable stir in her London street by painting her front door a particularly vivid pillar-box red.

Years ago, when I was a student living in digs in Paultons Square, Chelsea, I was fascinated by the way one could walk down a street of similar houses and suddenly spot, through a lighted window, an interior that looked really different, that seemed to say something interesting about the people who lived there. That was in the 1950s, a period of considerable conformity. Behind the scenes of London houses today there is a much more remarkable diversity.

When I was putting together my second house book more than 15 years ago, we included a feature that compared four houses located in the same north London terrace. From the outside, all the houses were pretty much the same, give or take an idiosyncratic taste in door colour. Inside, it was a different story. The basic structure and layout of the rooms were broadly similar, but each house nevertheless offered immense scope for personal expression.

The same is even truer today. Behind the Georgian façade of Richard Rogers' house in Chelsea, for example, there is an immaculate double-height modernist space; behind another Georgian façade in Spitalfields, home of the late historian Denis Severs, you will find an unnervingly accurate re-creation of eighteenth-century decor, complete with spluttering tallow candles. The most famous terraced house in London, 10 Downing Street, gives little hint from the outside of the Tardis-like extent of offices, staterooms and living accommodation within.

London's terraces have obviously survived because they satisfy a basic British need for personal territory, however circumscribed – the every-Englishman's-home-is-his-castle mentality, perhaps. But their survival must also stem from the fact that they can so easily be adapted as need and circumstance dictate. There are evidently many things you can do with a terraced house, and Londoners are increasingly prepared to do them (and planners to allow them). In some areas today the greatest drawback of living in a terraced street must be the constant noise of builders echoing through the party walls.

Rachel Whiteread, winner of the 1993 Turner Prize, caused a furore with *House*, a life-size concrete cast of a real house in Bow, east London. Unfortunately, her critics won and the evocative inside-out sculpture was demolished.

Over the past half-century the hidden diversity of London living has been increasingly matched by a more visible variety. Only a decade or so ago, it would have been difficult to predict the present popularity of 'loft living' and the willingness of so many Londoners to set up home in all kinds of redundant commercial and institutional buildings. Decommissioned churches, old schools, disused factories, offices and workshops now provide scope for much creative domestic energy.

A minority of Londoners have always lived in quirky places; someone has set up home on top of one of the towers of Tower Bridge, and the barges and houseboats of the Chelsea Embankment and Little Venice are further illustrations. Out of exigency or eccentricity, people have lived in tents, converted air-raid shelters, tree-houses, garages and huts – even in parked vehicles, as was the case for the playwright Alan Bennett's celebrated *Lady in the Van*. But the present vogue for adapting unconventional surroundings is largely new.

One could say that the trend owes much to the examples of New York artists' lofts or the colonizing of old merchants' canal warehouses in Amsterdam. It is true that similar demographic and economic conditions have prevailed in London, namely the departure of manufacturing from the inner city, releasing huge amounts of potentially liveable space at a time when space itself is one of the rarest of all commodities. As in New York, the vanguard has often been led by artists needing cheap studios and accommodation. But perhaps the fashion for loft living also reflects the fact that Londoners do not stay at home as much as they used to and are looking for more urban, central settings for their contemporary lifestyles.

In this respect, one of the biggest changes I have noticed about London in the past half-century is the change in people's aspirations. When I was young my contemporaries viewed living in London largely as a necessary evil and dreamed of one day having their own place in the country. Those for whom reality never quite met their expectations settled for the suburbs. Now it seems that people are more likely to dream of living in the thick of things in one of the newly fashionable inner-city areas buzzing with creative energy. Yesterday it was Clerkenwell, sandwiched between Islington and the City; today it is Hoxton in the heart of the East End; tomorrow it will be who knows where. And as big corporations discover that they no longer need headquarters in the centre of the city, there are some surprising new residential opportunities. Part of the Shell Centre, for example, situated right on the river, is currently being redeveloped into apartments.

I have lived in a variety of houses and flats in London, north and (just) south of the river, grand and grotty, from my parents' Hampstead house to student digs in Paultons Square, from a damp basement flat in Primrose Hill to the more elevated surroundings of a Georgian house

My commute to work involves walking down a flight of stairs – I live literally 'over the shop' on top of a building at Butlers Wharf designed by Michael Hopkins, where my design offices are located.

The Victorian warehouses at Butlers Wharf were once used to store spices.

in Regent's Park designed by Decimus Burton – albeit riddled with an active form of dry rot. Where I live now I like perhaps best of all. An apartment in a contemporary building designed by Michael Hopkins, it is resolutely modern in structure and layout. It is right on the river, directly above my office and design studios, and a stone's throw from both the Design Museum and the restaurants of Butlers Wharf. Best of all, there are ducks quacking on the river to wake you in the morning and no commuting to work.

The development of Butlers Wharf provides a good example of how neglected areas of the city can be revitalized. I first spotted the potential of the area in the 1980s, from a particularly good vantage point: the Thames. We had hired a pleasure boat for an office party and were cruising down the river when I noticed a wonderful collection of Victorian warehouses clustered on the south bank of the river alongside Tower Bridge. Although derelict and abandoned, these nineteenth-century commercial buildings had tremendous appeal, not to mention a terrific location just across the river from the City and the Tower of London.

When I looked at the area more closely, I became even more convinced of its potential. Until the Second World War, Butlers Wharf had been a thriving working area, where ships had unloaded their cargoes of spices, tea and coffee. After the war, when containerization spelled the end of London's docks, Butlers Wharf fell into a decline. In the succeeding decades, artists had occasionally attempted to set up studios in the decaying buildings but by the time I first visited the 12-acre site the only tenants claiming squatters' rights were the rats. More evocatively, I discovered that the streets and buildings – which I named Cardamom, Clove and Nutmeg – still smelled of the goods once stored there.

My vision for this derelict area was of a mixed-use community – places to live in, but also places to eat and shop in, along with a cultural draw, the Design Museum. I firmly believed that the area could be regenerated as successfully as had Covent Garden – until the mid-1970s a disused fruit and vegetable market knee-deep in rubbish, a decade or so later one of the most popular parts of central London. Conventional wisdom, needless to say, believed otherwise. I was told that money 'would never cross the river' (that old south London prejudice again), that City workers would never cross the river for lunch, much less dinner, and would certainly never dream of living there. Despite the sceptics, I formed a consortium of people to develop Butlers Wharf; we put together a scheme and we were eventually granted permission for a mixed-use development of apartments, shops, offices, restaurants and the Design Museum.

What subsequently happened is a long story. We had planned the development very carefully and invested heavily in the infrastructure, but had not budgeted for a very unpleasant discovery – Butlers Wharf itself, the main riverfront warehouse, had inadequate foundations. This proved extremely costly to remedy. Then the recession struck and the group was forced into receivership, like practically every other dockland developer at the time.

Today Butlers Wharf bustles with life again. Apartments in newly converted buildings or new structures sell out almost before they go on the market. The Design Museum is thriving and I am glad to say, as the owner of the restaurants and shops that make up the Butlers Wharf 'gastrodrome', that the sceptics have been proved wrong: people *will* cross the river, not only to eat, but also to shop, visit the museum and even set up home.

London living is not, however, an unmitigated success story, or a continuous process of rediscovery and regeneration with winners all round. I have been extremely fortunate, but anyone who lives in the capital cannot help but be aware that there are many who are not. Of the 33 most deprived boroughs in Britain, 14 are in London. It is estimated that nearly 80,000 Londoners have no permanent form of housing; at the extreme end of the spectrum are the rough sleepers who bed down on the streets and in shop doorways at night. At the same time, London as a whole has 120,000 empty houses, and it does not take much complex reckoning to see that there is an obvious solution here.

The scandal of so much empty space, while there are beggars on the streets, is enshrined in the name of London's charity for the homeless. Centrepoint, founded in 1969 in the crypt of St Anne's Church in Soho, takes its name from what was at that time London's most notorious empty space, the 35-storey office block Centre Point at the junction of Tottenham Court Road and Oxford Street. After it was completed in 1966 it stood vacant for 14 years, an anomaly that came to symbolize the unacceptable face of property development in the city – owing to a shortage of office space at the time, an empty building gained value at a greater rate than one that was occupied. A similar inequity can be seen in Camden where a new residential development of 'loft-style' apartments, the Glass Building, designed by Piers Gough of CZWG, has recently been finished. The new apartments, selling for hundreds of thousands of pounds, are right next door to Arlington House, Europe's largest shelter for the homeless.

Empty space is one thing, derelict space another. The architect Richard Rogers has estimated that five per cent of inner London is derelict. With millions of new homes required in Britain, many of them in the southeast, there is an urgent need to regenerate such urban 'brownfield' sites and avoid encroaching upon even more acres of unspoilt countryside.

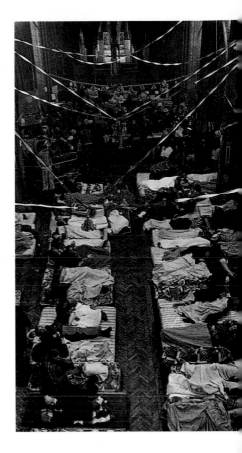

Initiatives such as Crisis at Christmas address the scandalous problem of London's homeless, desperate casualties of the property lottery.

There is another reason why such development should be encouraged. One of the elements I have always liked about London is its democratic quality. Until fairly recently most areas accommodated a blend of young and old, the better off and the not so well off. There are obvious exceptions, of course, but London has always seemed far more socially mixed than many other capitals. Recent rises in property prices have threatened this quality of integration. The current boom, which has seen, in just four years, house prices in some areas more than double, makes it very difficult for first-time buyers to break into the market and risks creating a dangerous polarization of rich and poor. People find they cannot afford to stay in the borough where they were born and grew up; teachers, nurses and other professionals in the service industries – key staff that London needs simply to keep going – increasingly find that they cannot afford to move to the capital at all. A recent comparative survey, based on the prices of a range of goods and services, has revealed that London is currently the most expensive city in the European Union, and the seventh most expensive in the world, after Tokyo, Osaka, Hong Kong, Libreville, Oslo and Zurich.

Addressing such problems means looking at new ways of providing affordable homes and tackling the decay and dereliction of certain parts of the inner city. In this context, an interesting development has been the successful regeneration of a number of old estates and tower blocks, which have until now been among the more conspicuous failures of town planning.

In the 1960s, when many tower blocks were built, the model for social housing was taken from Le Corbusier and his Unité d'Habitation. The idea of building 'streets in the sky' was to house as many people as possible while preserving the surrounding green space. When such schemes worked, they worked very well. Churchill Gardens in Pimlico, for example,. was designed in the late 1940s by the architects Powell and Moya, who went on to design the memorably iconic structure Skylon at the Festival of Britain. Comprising some 1,700 homes on a 30-acre site, Churchill Gardens was a model example of well-planned social housing. Shops, pubs, a school and a community centre were included in the development. Blocks of different heights were arranged around green areas where children could play. Each block had its own laundry and porter.

Churchill Gardens, however, was one of the few exceptions. Unfortunately for London, as for many other cities in Britain, several critical factors tended to be left out of the equation when it came to the design of public-sector housing. The tower blocks were often poorly built, with substandard materials, which meant they fell apart quickly. Communal features, the humanizing elements of Le Corbusier schemes – such as laundries, nurseries and crèches, porterage, shops and sports facilities – were generally omitted on grounds of cost. Poorly run, badly maintained and with no security, the London tower block rapidly became a no-go area, more akin to a ghetto than a community.

Recent schemes have proved that the trend can be reversed. Repairing the physical fabric of the buildings is a necessary preliminary, but sometimes the simple action of providing tower blocks with their own concierges has led to a sharp decline in crime and vandalism. Trellick Tower in north Kensington, designed by Ernö Goldfinger, has seen such a reversal of fortune. Less than a decade ago it was a notorious housing black spot. Dubbed 'Colditz in the Sky' by some newspapers, it was riddled with crime and filled with problem families. The lifts did not work, the corridors stank and there was a two-year waiting list to be rehoused. Nowadays the shoe is on the other foot, with people queuing up for a chance to live in one of the flats.

What happened to change the situation? An improvement came with the foundation of a residents' association for Trellick Tower to promote the building's architectural assets, the thoughtful planning, well-proportioned spaces and the quality of the detailing. Their efforts gradually had an effect on council policy. Only those who wanted to live in Trellick were offered flats there. A new boiler and new lifts were installed, a playground was created and, most important of all, 24-hour security was provided. (When Trellick first opened, in 1972, the plan to have a concierge in the lobby was quashed by the GLC, which viewed such an arrangement as overly authoritarian.) Once considered a monstrous blot on the west London landscape, the building has recently been listed.

Regeneration offers the opportunity to rebuild from the inside and creates a chance to reverse the trend whereby rising prices push people further from the centre. Richard Rogers, who argues in favour of using urban land at higher densities rather than gobbling up acres of countryside with low-rise and low-density development, has estimated that 570,000 new homes could be built in London on previously used or brownfield sites. I agree with him. This, in turn, would help to breathe new life into the city's communities and halt the flight from the centre. According to figures produced by the London Planning Advisory Committee, there is room for up to half a million new homes eastwards along the river corridor – a development that will inevitably be spurred by the fact that, with the new Jubilee Line Extension, it is now easy to get there. Those who study the London property market report that people who move east tend to be young, creative and more likely to eat out … Living in London, like everything else about the city, is all set to change in exciting ways.

One way to solve the problem. 'Blow-downs' – demolition of high-rise blocks – make room for more popular low-rise public housing.

OVERLEAF: Churchill Gardens, Pimlico, was designed by Powell and Moya. The estate includes shops, pubs, a school and a community centre; its sensitive planning, mixture of high- and low-rise housing and essential optimism make it a model of good practice.

Despite the terrace pattern, London living is surprisingly diverse. Few homes are as grand as those in **Park Crescent**, the colonnaded semicircle designed by **John Nash** (RIGHT). When your house is in the same style as your neighbour's, colour can be a way of expressing individuality (ABOVE). London's network of canals are increasingly popular places to set up home (LEFT). A narrowboat makes an economical, if compact, living space.

Modern design may have been a minority taste until recently but it has quite a respectable London history. The Cheyne Walk home, where British designers Robin and Lucienne Day have lived since the early 1950s, still looks remarkably fresh and contemporary today (ABOVE LEFT). This interior of one of the flats in Golden Lane Estate (LEFT), designed by Chamberlin, Powell & Bon in the 1950s, reveals pleasing proportions and a high quality of material finish. Many examples of London's postwar social housing were inspired by Le Corbusier's Unité d'Habitation; Golden Lane is one of the few intelligent and successful interpretations.

RIGHT AND BELOW RIGHT:
Ernö Goldfinger's Hampstead
home, 2 Willow Road, built in
the 1930s, was once reviled by
local residents. James Bond's
creator Ian Fleming was one
of Goldfinger's neighbours and
openly contested his
applications for planning
permission, which may
account for the fact that
'Goldfinger' is a notorious
Bond villain. Today the house
is run by the National Trust
and visited by hundreds of
architectural aficionados.
Decades before loft living,
Goldfinger created flexible
living space with sliding
partitions.

The regeneration of run-down areas of the city often owes a great deal to artists, who are prepared to accept a little decay in exchange for cheap accommodation and studio space. Warehouses, such as Metropolitan Wharf (TOP LEFT) and mews, such as Chippenham Mews (ABOVE LEFT) are building types that are ripe for recycling. Dilapidated terraces with unfashionable postcodes – such as Brick Lane (TOP RIGHT) or Beck Road in Hackney (ABOVE RIGHT) – have become artists' enclaves. The community of artists, writers and film-makers based in a Georgian house near the British Museum keeps the Bloomsbury spirit alive (RIGHT).

PREVIOUS PAGES: Israeli-born designer Ron Arad in his Belsize
Park home (LEFT). Men's couturier Oswald Boateng relaxes in his
red, orange and fuchsia study in Wimpole Street (RIGHT).

London, like all big cities, provides scope for reinventing yourself, or simply reinventing your surroundings, whether this entails installing a swing in the living room (FAR LEFT), getting inventive with a bedstead (LEFT) or customizing a kitchen (TOP LEFT AND ABOVE).

Designed by Andrew Martin, the White House in Holland Park provides a radical
redefinition of the mews, with open-plan garaging (BELOW). Rock star and
LiveAid organiser Bob Geldof at home in his Chelsea apartment (RIGHT).

PREVIOUS PAGES: Bicycles line the hallway of a communal artists' house in Bloomsbury (LEFT). Ground-floor corridor of
Number 10 Downing Street, London's best-known address (RIGHT).

First built as the London house of Viscount Melbourne, Albany on Piccadilly was converted by Henry Holland in 1802 into 69 sets of private chambers. Residents have included Byron, Aldous Huxley, Lord Snowdon, Graham Greene and Edward Heath as well as the late interior designer David Hicks, whose bedroom shown here was decorated in 1981 (LEFT). The decision of Derry Irvine, the present Lord Chancellor, to redecorate his official residence with historically correct hand-blocked wallpaper has proved controversial to say the least (RIGHT).

PREVIOUS PAGES: Performance artists Gilbert and George live in a Georgian house off Commercial Street situated between a church and a mosque (LEFT), in their words 'the most up-to-date cosmological place on earth'. A taste for the macabre informs the decoration of this Gothic Kentish Town flat, home of a New Zealand-born graphic designer (RIGHT).

Jimi Hendrix has one. So does Boris Karloff, Dame Sybil Thorndike and Sir Winston Churchill; Byron had the first. Blue plaques, commemorating places associated with famous people, were initiated by the Royal Society of Arts in 1867; there are now 700 of these discreet markers across London. Michael Palin poses with a (temporary) blue plaque at a laundrette in the Uxbridge Road, the location for an early Monty Python sketch (RIGHT).

The Chelsea home of architect Richard Rogers and his wife Ruth, co-owner of the River Café, features a soaring double-height light-filled living/dining/cooking area behind the rather more conventional façade of a Georgian house (LEFT AND FAR LEFT). A terraced property in Ladbroke Grove has seen a similarly radical transformation, with a clean-lined contemporary space carved out of a basement area (ABOVE).

The sheer scale of industrial spaces offers the potential for new ways of living and working. This top-floor loft in Shoreditch serves as home and studio for artist Abigail Lane, but also accommodates a host of other activities, functioning part of the time as a hairdresser's salon, rehearsal space and as a venue for art events and parties.

Home is where the art is. For the residents of Trellick Tower (LEFT), this meant participation in *Breathing In and Breathing Out*, a lightwork by sculptor Ron Haselden working in collaboration with architect Robert Barnes. As the residents changed coloured gels placed on top of lights on their balconies, the tower rippled with a mosaic of light patterns (ABOVE).

Maggie Ellenby's shop window opposite Sadler's Wells theatre, located within a residential street, is the venue for a sequence of mysterious window displays that pique the curiosity of passers-by: *After Dark, Part I,* 1993 (TOP LEFT), *Wood I,* 1995 (CENTRE LEFT) and *Diamonds Forever,* 1999 (BELOW LEFT). Installations change after an indeterminate length of time in what the artist describes as a 'long, drawn-out tease'.

Transport

One of the panel games on the popular long-running Radio 4 comedy quiz show *I'm Sorry, I Haven't a Clue* is called 'Mornington Crescent'. The point of the game is that there isn't one. Panellists call out names of London Tube stations in turn, pretending to follow non-existent rules: Tooting Bec, Ealing Broadway, Bank, Moorgate, Willesden Green, and so on, until someone triumphantly announces 'Mornington Crescent' and the game is over. Mornington Crescent is a station on the Northern Line famous for being closed for years, but which reopened, gleamingly modernized, in April 1998 after a protracted period of refurbishment.

LEFT: Vaulted glass roof at Canary Wharf station on the Docklands Light Railway.

In recent years getting around London has increasingly felt like a game of Mornington Crescent that has gone badly wrong. Part of the attraction of the radio game is the way it seems to express an underlying affection for the Tube, the public-transport network that Londoners depend upon more than any other. Today, however, that affection is fraying somewhat around the edges, to put it mildly. The Northern Line earned its nickname the Misery Line quite some time ago – although things have improved lately with the introduction of new, and more frequent, carriages. Nevertheless, the rising numbers of train cancellations, signal failures, broken escalators and overcrowded carriages have all served to spread the misery to other lines as well, not to mention the commuter services coming into the great railway terminals of Waterloo, Victoria, Paddington, Liverpool Street and King's Cross. At the faintest whisper of snow or the 'wrong' sort of leaves on the track, the whole antiquated and underinvested system comes juddering to a halt. More than many other major cities, London is particularly dependent on its rail links and shortfalls are acutely felt. With more than one million commuters coming into the city every working day and between a quarter and half a million using each Underground line, there is the potential to upset a lot of people.

ABOVE: The bar and circle logo of London Underground provides an instantly recognizable point of orientation. The sign was designed by Edward Johnston, who was also responsible for the lettering used throughout the system.

It is not just commuters who have noticed the decline. Recent guidebooks to London, in both the *Rough Guide* and *Lonely Planet* series, have singled out the poor standard of public transport for criticism. The *Rough Guide* describes the Tube as near 'breaking point' and London buses as 'notoriously unreliable'. The *Lonely Planet* guide notes that London drivers are 'aggressive in the extreme' and that Londoners generally are much ruder than they used to be. I would hazard a guess that the two observations are related. Even a nation as characteristically phlegmatic as the British will eventually lose its collective cool when subject to daily delays and overcrowding in the process of simply getting from A to B.

The unreliability of public transport has had the predictable effect of forcing more and more people to take to their cars. The result is that at peak hours many streets of the city now resemble a war zone, where cars battle it out with freewheeling cyclists, weaving motorbike messengers, the ubiquitous white delivery vans, taxis and beleaguered buses. Two-thirds of all journeys in London are now made by car. Pollution, in consequence, is also at record levels. Eight out of the ten most polluted streets in Britain are in central London.

Most London jams are simply the effect of 'sheer volume of traffic', a depressingly familiar phrase for commuters. Others are conspicuously due to the plague of roadworks that has descended on the capital since the privatization of the main utilities companies. It seems that no sooner has a gas company finished with a particular stretch of road than a cable company arrives and proceeds to dig fresh holes in it – holes (or 'street openings' to use the corporate euphemism) that, to many drivers stuck stationary in traffic, seem almost insolently unattended nine-tenths of the time. I would like to suggest that our new Mayor look carefully at the system under which organizations gain permission to carry out these works, so that the activities can be properly coordinated. I would go further, in fact, and charge companies by the hour and by metre of road, with punitive fines if original estimates are exceeded.

A traffic controller keeps tabs on the 30 million vehicles that use the Dartford Tunnel and QEII Bridge each year, with the aid of 37 television monitors.

With the proliferation of such roadworks and of one-way systems in residential areas, the average driver increasingly needs the 'Knowledge' of a London cabbie to avoid the main routes successfully. Busy junctions, such as the Hanger Lane gyratory system or London's most notorious roundabout, Hyde Park Corner, can gridlock in a matter of minutes if a single vehicle stalls or breaks down and the knock-on effect can take hours to untangle.

Traffic managers cannot do much about the volume, but they can endeavour to prevent standstills and keep traffic flowing, albeit slowly. In 1997 a traffic-signals engineer called Stuart Beniston 'found' seven seconds going spare at Hanger Lane, a complex roundabout that controls the junction between one of the busiest routes out of London, the A40, and the North Circular, one of London's oldest ring roads. Nearly 8,000 vehicles per hour use the gyratory system. Using a computer model Beniston analysed the sequences of the various traffic lights around the system, discovered the spare seconds and redesigned the traffic plan to incorporate them where they were needed. The result was an immediate improvement, but not a solution.

Something similar has happened at Hyde Park Corner, long one of London's true white-knuckle rides and the scene of many spectacular jams. Again, traffic engineers using a computer model have analysed the rhythm of the traffic to discover precisely where the hold-ups were occurring, and introduced new traffic lights and lane markings to improve matters. There is no less traffic – 100,000 vehicles a day, on average – but it now flows more freely, sometimes.

Shaving seconds off traffic cycles, however, is akin to rearranging deck chairs on the *Titanic*. As roads grow ever more congested, journey times lengthen and pollution rises, a sort of vicious circle comes into play. The more cars there are on the road, the more people fear traffic. Road safety is a prime concern for parents, who increasingly drive their children everywhere rather than allow them to make the journey on foot or by public transport. Some see the growth in numbers of commuters who have opted to drive to work as being responsible for London's log jam, but the relative peace of certain London streets during the school holidays indicates that the school run must be at least partly to blame. The fear of traffic is not misplaced: in the first six months of 1999 there was a 25 per cent increase in the number of road deaths in the capital.

There are also several psychological factors at work. Even when the traffic is at a stand-still, people still regard cars as a convenience, their private territory. This stems from that old British domestic ideal of one's own front door, garden and parking space. And once people have lost the habit of taking public transport, it is increasingly difficult to win them back.

Given this state of affairs, it is small wonder that the future of London transport has become a key issue for the new Mayor. How to finance new Underground lines and rail links, as well as carry out necessary improvements and repairs to existing ones; whether or not to save the Routemaster, London's beloved double-decker; and what restrictions to place on drivers in the capital are all subjects for heated debate.

I am not a politician, and consequently I do not have to come up with a definitive answer for such problems or produce a detailed breakdown of how I would fund my proposals. However, with my experience of visiting other cities I would say that when it comes to dealing with cars Paris has got it about right. In Paris many open spaces have car parks underneath; people simply do not expect to park on the street. It is, of course, more costly to create underground parking, but it removes congestion from the streets without rendering them completely lifeless.

As a designer, I would also direct attention back to the period before the Second World War when public transport in London was the most progressive in the world and a real source of civic pride. This happy situation was achieved not only by political commitment but also by the visionary use of design to create a memorable corporate identity for what was, and still is, an essential part of the city's infrastructure.

The first Underground line – Baker Street to Farringdon – opened in 1863. In the decades that followed, Underground lines and stations were constructed throughout the capital in what amounted to a frenzy of speculative building. The first London-wide elected body, the London County Council, was established in 1888. An early aim was to take services such as gas, electricity, water – and transport – into municipal ownership. This took some time and it was not until the early 1930s that London bus, tram, rail and Underground services were fully integrated. An ambitious design programme spelled out the unity of the new public system. Much of the credit for this visual identity can be laid at the door of one man, Frank Pick.

Frank Pick was much influenced by the ideals of William Morris and others in the Arts and Crafts movement, which were concerned with bringing art and design into the everyday experience of ordinary people. When Pick was Commercial Manager of the London Underground he commissioned the calligrapher and typographer Edward Johnston to create a new typeface for all the signage to be used throughout the system. The Johnston lettering for London Underground, an elegant sans-serif face, was designed in 1916. A variation of Johnston is still in use today, as defining a characteristic of the Tube as Art Nouveau-style lettering is of the Paris Métro. Edward Johnston also designed the 'bar and circle' logo, one of the most recognizable of all London symbols.

After the transport services were integrated, Pick became the Chief Executive of London Underground, and carried on his programme of modernization. He commissioned the architect Charles Holden to design new stations on the network and redesign old ones: Boston Manor and Arnos Grove are two outstanding examples of Holden's work, as is the ticket hall at Piccadilly Circus, beautifully detailed in brass and wood. Holden was a modernist and a functionalist, much influenced by the Bauhaus; the purpose of the new stations was to provide a sense of visual coherence for the publicly owned network.

The 'Diagram', the innovative Tube map produced by Harry Beck, dates from around this time. Instead of producing a geographically accurate plan of the system, Beck's brainwave was to make a map that showed the relationships between stations and lines in a way that was

Arnos Grove on the Piccadilly Line is an outstanding example of the work of Charles Holden, the architect commissioned by Frank Pick in the 1930s to design new stations and update existing ones.

easy to understand, using colour to represent the different Tube lines: black for the Northern Line, yellow for the Circle, red for the Central and so on. (In fact, the Circle Line is not truly a line at all, but employs sections of the District, Hammersmith and City and Metropolitan Lines to create its circular route around the inner areas of the capital.)

No detail was too small for Pick. Leading designers such as Enid Marx produced textile designs for the moquette fabric which covered the seats of the carriages. Modern artists such as Man Ray were engaged to produce designs for posters encouraging people to travel by Tube. In the early 1930s the *RIBA Journal* did not stint its praise: 'That the directors of the Underground Railway should have so correlated every part of their organization that everything from a poster or a doorknob to a complete station should so clearly express "Underground" is an achievement of which they have good reason to be proud.'

The effect of all this activity was to spell out the message of quality and thoughtfulness. The transport system, with its clear signage, exciting new stations and bright public face, was not a second-rate alternative to getting around the city above ground: it was the only way to travel. The fact that soon after these transformations were complete the Tube was adopted as a safe haven by those sheltering from the Blitz only strengthened its hold on the public's affections. (Interestingly though, at the beginning of the raids Londoners were instructed not to shelter in Underground stations. What followed was a popular revolt: people simply bought a cheap ticket and went down to the Tube anyway. The authorities finally gave in.)

Today, the transport network as a whole does not offer quite the same cause for metropolitan pride. But I am essentially an optimist, even where London's transport problems are concerned. One conspicuous reason to be cheerful is the new Jubilee Line Extension. For the first time in many, many years here is a development that displays both foresight and positive spirit, qualities in fairly short supply since the days of Frank Pick. Travelling on the new line is a joy: the trains run smoothly, if still a little unreliably, and everything fits together so well that there is no need to 'mind the gap', thanks to the new glazed double-barriers between carriages and platforms. The stations are fantastic. It is hard to pick a favourite … the soaring cathedral-like vault of Canary Wharf, the shimmering blue mosaic of North Greenwich or the curving reflective glass wall of Southwark?

The Tube map created by Harry Beck, known as the 'Diagram', is a model of clarity and user-friendliness. You know that a design has become an institution when artists start to have fun with it. Simon Patterson's *The Great Bear* (1992) features 'lines' of philosophers, constellations, actors ….

Roland Paoletti has been the architect in charge of overseeing the design of the new line. Unlike Frank Pick, who sought to provide a single unified identity, Paoletti adopted the contrasting strategy of commissioning a different architect for each new station (11 in all), including Norman Foster (Canary Wharf), Chris Wilkinson (Stratford), Ron Herron (Canada Water), Alsop and Stormer (North Greenwich), Richard MacCormac (Southwark) and Michael Hopkins (Westminster). Although each station reveals an individual design approach, there are certain common themes. Many of them are vast. Canary Wharf is designed to handle 40,000 passengers per hour at peak times; One Canada Square, the tower at Canary Wharf that dominates the skyline of east London, could fit inside, laid flat. North Greenwich is the largest underground station in Europe. Even the smaller stations have the same airy feeling of generosity, a quality pretty much lacking in most of the rest of the Underground. Although the platforms are deep, the structures have been designed and engineered so that natural light filters down from above. As is the case with the much-maligned Dome, the creative partnership of architecture and engineering is striking.

The JLE may have been notoriously late and, at a total cost of £3.5 billion, vastly over-budget, but now that it is open it is destined to play a critical role in the city's eastwards shift, bringing new prosperity to areas that were formerly moribund. But I believe the quality of its design will also serve to raise people's expectations of what London's transport system could and should be like in the future.

Like many people who live in London, I am fascinated by the secret parts of the city, the sense that something mysterious may be happening just around the corner, or that you may suddenly stumble on an alleyway you never knew existed. Many of London's best-kept secrets are underground. There are more than 40 redundant stations, thrown up in the Victorian rush for development but subsequently closed, often owing to underuse. These can occasionally be glimpsed as a train speeds along a tunnel, or detected overground in the characteristic arched brickwork of former entrances. One closed station, Down Street, near Hyde Park Corner, was where Churchill and his Cabinet sheltered during the war. Eisenhower had his base in the tunnels of Goodge Street station; Eisenhower Tower is an upside-down 32-storey structure off Tottenham Court Road that is now run by a company offering secure storage for archives. There are reputed to be some 12 miles of secret underground tunnels and bunkers crisscrossing the city, designed to serve as emergency headquarters for government departments in the case of nuclear war. During the Zeppelin raids of the First World War the Elgin Marbles were temporarily stored in the underground tunnels of the Post Office's miniature railway, a network of seven stations running from Whitechapel in the east to Paddington. The romance and mystery of these secret locations has a powerful appeal. Aldwych station, which closed in 1994, has served in recent years as an evocative venue for private parties, fashion shoots and degree shows.

Buried under London are also 35,000 miles of sewers, possibly the single most important transport system in the city. The original scheme was devised by the great Victorian engineer Joseph Bazalgette, but was only adopted after the 'Great Stink' of 1858 when the Thames, then more or less a gigantic cesspool, smelled so dire that Parliament had to remove itself temporarily from the nauseating stench wafting up from the riverbank. Bazalgette's brilliant notion was to exploit the natural gradient of the London basin in the design of the new sewage system. The brick-built sewers, constructed in the 1860s, were a miracle of nineteenth-century engineering; their role in promoting public health and removing the scourge of disease from the city laid the foundations for the modern capital.

Perhaps the most poignant underground features are London's lost rivers, tributaries of the Thames such as the Fleet, the Walbrook and the Westbourne that once trickled through the city but are now trapped beneath the pavements. Some have been used as sewers but most simply cause problems for London Underground engineers, who have to ensure that millions of gallons of water are constantly pumped away so that Tube stations and tunnels remain free from flooding.

Until recently it would not have been too fanciful to characterize the Thames itself as a 'lost' river, certainly as one whose role had been temporarily mislaid. Anyone who has been to see *Shakespeare in Love*, or the much earlier British film success *A Man for All Seasons*, cannot fail to appreciate the central role the river used to play as London's central thoroughfare, with ferrymen taking passengers from bank to bank or back and forth between the seats of power at Westminster and Greenwich. For centuries there was only one bridge across the Thames – or rather a succession of bridges at the same crossing point – and river traffic provided an essential way of getting about. In those days, the river was a wide, shallow and slow-moving waterway, which made it easy to navigate. In later centuries, as more and more land was reclaimed from the Thames and the Embankments were built, the profile of the river altered radically, becoming a narrower, deeper, swifter and much more hazardous channel.

In Tudor, Stuart and Georgian times the river was also the setting for royal spectacles and pageantry; when it froze over from time to time during the 'Little Ice Age' of the sixteenth and seventeenth centuries it was the scene of those great public festivities, the

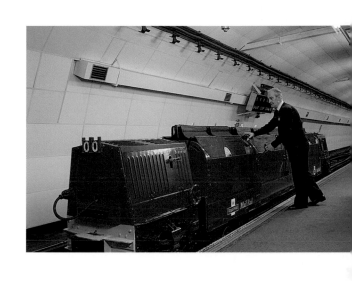

Seven stations from Whitechapel to Paddington comprise the underground network of the Post Office railway, one of London's hidden lines of communication.

The gleaming steel shells of the Thames Barrier span the river at Woolwich, where ten gates regulate the tidal flow. The barrier was designed by engineers Rendel, Palmer and Tritton and built between 1975 and 1982. To me, the organic form of these massive gates finds a strong echo in Frank Gehry's design for the Guggenheim Museum in Bilbao.

Frost Fairs. It is no accident that the river offers the best and grandest views of some of London's finest monuments, such as the Houses of Parliament, the Tower of London and the Royal Naval College in Greenwich.

But first and foremost the Thames was a river of trade. At the turn of the eighteenth century more than three-quarters of all imports into England came via the Thames. Docks, wharves and warehouses clustered thickly along the banks. By the 1930s the bustling port of London employed more than 100,000 people, and 1,000 ships per week were still arriving in the mid-1950s.

After the Second World War, however, the river abruptly lost its commercial role. In the late 1960s containerization completed the job begun by the bombs of Hitler's Luftwaffe, and the docks stood empty and derelict. Although the redevelopment of Docklands in the 1980s with its gleaming office blocks, riverside housing and toy-town railway started the process of regenerating the industrial wastelands along the Thames corridor, the river itself failed to come alive. That is, except in the most literal sense: once foul and murky, the Thames is now so clean that salmon have returned to the river, along with many other species of fish and waterfowl.

Over the past few years there has been a growing awareness of the potential of the river, not only as a means of connecting the north and south, east and west of the city, but also as the symbolic heart of the capital. The changing nature of shipping and the departure of heavy industry from London inevitably mean that the Thames will never return to its former use as an industrial waterway, but those of us who remember the filthy, dirty Thames of old, crowded with coal barges, may well think that that is no bad thing. What can be recovered, however, is the river's role as a main artery. For this to happen proper river-transport systems are required, integrated into the existing infrastructure.

A kick-start to this process is already under way in the regeneration of the south bank of the Thames. The 'string of pearls' concept of bringing the river to life by developing key points along it, an idea often articulated by Richard Rogers, is no longer wishful thinking. For years the entire portion of the southeast bank between Tower Bridge and the South Bank Centre – home of the Festival Hall, Hayward Gallery and National Theatre – was a cultural desert, and a fairly inaccessible one at that, with little apparent connection to the other side of the river. Now Bankside, as the area has now come to be known, has undergone an architectural and cultural makeover. Tate Modern, housed in a defunct power station;

Shakespeare's Globe, a replica of the original Elizabethan theatre; and the new scheme to give a facelift to the South Bank Centre itself have brought about a revival of the area's fortunes. The reversal had already begun with the regeneration of Gabriel's Wharf and Coin Street, and the conversion of the Oxo Tower into a mixed-use development of restaurants, studios, workshops and affordable housing. More commercial and residential schemes are planned.

Transport has played a key role in the Bankside renaissance. The new London Bridge and Southwark stations on the JLE reunite the area with central London. The swinging Millennium Footbridge, designed by my old friends Norman Foster and Antony Caro, elegantly spans the river between St Paul's and Tate Modern, incidentally connecting one of the capital's richest boroughs, the City, with one of its poorest, Southwark. New jetties and piers support a riverbus service, with operators ferrying visitors to the Dome further downstream throughout the millennial year and, we hope, for years to come.

This latter initiative is particularly interesting. River transport services have been tried before, but have not succeeded. There are several reasons for this. The first is that previous schemes were never very well publicized and were not properly integrated into existing London transport links – Londoners only took to them when all else failed, such as during Tube strikes, for example. That problem has now been addressed with the new piers sited within easy access of the new JLE stations. The second problem is economic and has to do with the nature of the Thames itself. The ebb and flow of the tidal Thames means that riverboats have to use a great deal of fuel on the legs of the journeys when they are running against the tide, which in turn means that they are expensive to operate. Like some others, I feel that a solution might be to use the Thames Barrier to control the ebb and flow and keep the river artificially high. But, as environmentalists point out, there is an ecological cost to this, which is the loss of natural habitats for fish and waterfowl in the intertidal reaches of the Thames. Yet even if riverboats never quite replace the Tube as the commuter's preferred method of transportation, I am certain that they will find a secure role simply as one of the most pleasant ways that visitors and tourists – or simply Londoners on their days off – can appreciate the city.

The shift south and east of the capital's centre of gravity means that it may be time to look again at the idea of building a fifth London airport. Personally, I would like to see Maplin Sands reconsidered as a possible site. Locating an airport east of the city would close the economic gap between central London and Docklands for good, and provide a powerful spur for the regeneration of the entire Thames corridor. After all, only 50 years ago Heath Row was an obscure village to the west of London....

OVERLEAF: **With 23 ticket barriers and a mountainous bank of escalators, everything about Canary Wharf station on the Jubilee Line by Foster and Partners is grand in scale – it is so vast that it could accommodate the whole of the tower at Canada Square (LEFT). London's network of Victorian sewers was originally devised by the great engineer Joseph Bazalgette (RIGHT).**

Forming the frontage to St Pancras station, the former Midland Grand Hotel, now St Pancras
Chambers, was designed by George Gilbert Scott and completed in 1892 (ABOVE) – 'possibly too good
for its purpose' in the architect's own estimation. After its closure in 1935 the hotel, which had 250
bedrooms and featured the first ladies' smoking room in London, was converted for use as offices.
The magnificent Gothic staircase (RIGHT) and other parts of the interior can be viewed on London
Open House weekends, an annual opportunity to visit buildings not normally open to the public.

The Westway, the elevated portion of the A40 which forms one of the capital's main gateways, opened 30 years ago. At any time, one in fifteen drivers in London is said to be lost, a fairly sobering thought that highlights the fact that signage should be improved.

London Bridge – or rather a succession of bridges in the same spot – was the only crossing point on the Thames until 1750. Tower Bridge, which is below London Bridge, was designed by Sir Horace Jones and opened in 1894 (LEFT). This is a 'bascule' bridge, which means that its central sections can be lifted to allow ships to pass through – one of the great sights of London. If Tower Bridge is one of the city's best-loved, Albert Bridge (ABOVE), linking Chelsea with Battersea, must be one of the most beautiful, with its three pairs of ornamental cast-iron towers. It opened in 1873.

London's Millennium Footbridge, designed by Foster and Partners, sculptor Antony Caro and engineers Ove Arup, opened with a bad case of the wobbles. Conceived as a 'blade of light' linking the City with the South Bank, it is the longest horizontal suspension bridge in the world.

In certain parts of central London, rush hour now lasts all day, with routes such as Oxford Street at a standstill and buses crammed to capacity (LEFT). Faced with this type of daily congestion, it is small wonder that many Londoners are keen to explore the potential of alternative modes of transportation (ABOVE).

A day in the life of the 38 bus, which carries seven and a half million passengers a year between Clapton and Victoria. New buses may be safer (no falling off the back platform) and easier to access with their low floors, but the remaining Routemasters inspire much affection. The Routemaster was designed so that damaged parts could be unbolted and replaced easily; the bus has proved the true workhorse of London transport.

OVERLEAF: Fly-past of **AA** helicopters.

To coin a phrase, the new Jubilee Line stations are 'cathedrals' of transport. Although each is designed by a different architect, they all share a quality of lightness and spaciousness, a generosity of scale very different from the average cramped tube station. TOP, FROM LEFT TO RIGHT: Canada Water, Southwark, North Greenwich. BELOW, FROM LEFT TO RIGHT: Canary Wharf, London Bridge.

ABOVE: Waterloo International Terminal, home of the Eurostar, was designed by Nicholas Grimshaw in 1994. Its sinuous glass roof provides a modern update of a characteristic feature of Victorian station design.

RIGHT: Clarity and spaciousness are the hallmarks of another Grimshaw design, the recent reworking of Paddington station, originally designed by the great Isambard Kingdom Brunel and constructed between 1850 and 1854.

OVERLEAF: **A river runs through it … and a ring road runs round it. A** heavily congested **M25**, London's orbital (RIGHT), contrasts with the most underused of the capital's routes, the Thames (LEFT).

Work

There are many world-class cities that are not capitals – one has only to consider Sydney, Barcelona, Hong Kong or New York. Similarly, there are many capitals that are not commercial centres – Ottawa and Canberra, for example, do not dominate the economic life of their respective countries. London, however, has always been both a centre of business and a centre of power. These twin engines make a formidable driving force.

To a large extent, the two major aspects of working London – commerce and power – have also shaped the development of the city. The geography of the city makes explicit the two competing spheres of influence. Westminster, the home of court and government, was sited outside the original city walls. Inside the walls was the mercantile heart of the capital where the guilds and livery companies established their stronghold. Today, this famous Square Mile is home to the City of London, the financial powerhouse that pulsates to a global beat. There are fewer than 6,000 true residents of the City, but a quarter of a million flood into the area every day to work in the banks and multinational corporations that tower above its streets.

Some of London's most memorable architectural landmarks were designed first and foremost as places of work. In this respect, I find the City intensely fascinating. Its warren-like nature, and the sudden contrast of new and old, constantly throw up surprises. The Lloyd's Building, with its forthright display of external servicing, is not too distant from the Bank of England, the 'Grand Old Lady of Threadneedle Street', whose windowless lower storey is all that remains of Sir John Soane's original eighteenth-century design. Hidden away down City lanes, tucked between unremarkable or remarkably awful 1960s office blocks, are the splendours of the old livery company halls, a few of which date back to the seventeenth century. Next door to Smithfield meat market is London's oldest hospital, St Bartholomew's, or Bart's, founded in 1123. The staircase of the Great Hall, part of the hospital designed by James Gibbs in the eighteenth century, is decorated with murals painted by Hogarth. Such provocative juxtapositions are not unique to the City – they occur London-wide – but in the City the effect is much more intense and compressed. Until fairly recently the whole area was more or less dead at night and at weekends; now, with traders arriving at their desks early or staying late to catch the financial markets halfway

LEFT: **Every day is Take Your Dog to Work Day in this Kentish Town graphic design studio.**

round the world just as they open or before they close, there is much more vitality in the streets. Because of this, more restaurants, cafés and bars have opened and the City is now beginning to resemble the West End in its level of evening activity.

Working buildings, of course, often have life spans tied into their particular function. Lawyers still practise from chambers in the Inns of Court; private doctors still operate from consulting rooms in Harley Street. But with the advent of computer typesetting and digital technology, Fleet Street ceased to be home to the national press and most of the warehouses and workshops of industrial London have fallen vacant as manufacturing has quit the city. One of the biggest changes of all has been the trend for home-working. The past decade has seen a tenfold increase in the number of people in Britain working from home, a trend that will undoubtedly continue and probably escalate.

Uncut £5 note sheets arrive at the Bank of England for examination. It is estimated that by 2002 London will be the seventh-largest economy in Europe.

London as a whole has some 250,000 businesses, employing 3.3 million people. Its gross domestic product is expected to top £200 billion in the next year or so, which will make it the seventh-largest economy in Europe. In 1999 40,000 new businesses were started in the city and, according to the Chancellor of the Exchequer, unemployment was at its lowest for 20 years. By anyone's reckoning, this amounts to a quite considerable degree of economic success. But what the figures conceal is the fundamental shift in the way Londoners work today, compared with 10 or 20 years ago.

When I was first setting up in business, no City gent was without his bowler hat and tightly furled umbrella. The dress code was rigid. I had a bowler hat myself, which I dusted down and wore on the occasions when I had to see my bank manager. I did not like the hat, but I simply would not have been taken seriously by the powers that be without one. Nowadays much of that starchy formality has gone, and laptops and mobile phones have replaced the umbrella as essential accessories. While it is still not quite a case of anything goes, the more relaxed style of dress of the average office worker, not merely on 'dress-down Fridays', is symbolic of a greater fluidity in the nature of work itself.

Working London has experienced radical changes over the past few decades, changes that technological developments have only accelerated. One of the first was the sudden decline of London as a port in the 1960s, which meant that thousands of working-class jobs disappeared overnight. Around the same time it was official policy to encourage manufacturing to move out of the city. When I was looking to expand my furniture-making business at the beginning of the 1960s I was given a grant by what was then the LCC to build a new factory – in Thetford, Norfolk. So I closed my two factories in Camberwell and Fulham and took 80 London families to live and work in the country. London was far from unique in this respect. Many big corporations moved their headquarters out of Manhattan in the 1960s and 1970s, seeking a better quality of life in the surrounding suburban areas. In the early 1970s we opened our first American Habitat store in the new Citicorp Building, which was the only new office block being built in New York at that time.

No change has affected London quite like the loss of its industries. London was always a city not only of trade but of manufacture, traditionally producing luxury or high-value goods for a ready metropolitan market. When the Great Exhibition opened in 1851 in the gleaming Crystal Palace, it provided a showcase for the huge variety of products made in what was then the largest industrial city in the world. Many of these goods were associated with specific areas. Bermondsey was the centre of the leather trade; the area around Tottenham Court Road was known for high-quality furniture, while cheaper furniture was made in Stepney and Shoreditch. Watches and clocks were made in Clerkenwell; silk was woven in Bethnal Green, where the Huguenots had settled. There were potteries in Lambeth, hatters in Southwark, wood-workers and shipbuilders along the Thames. By the end of the century these small workshop-based industries had been joined by larger mills and factories. South London produced glass, beer, soap, glue, dye, bleach and paint, while the estuarine pastures of the east Thames corridor became the home of gasworks and chemical industries.

Between the wars, even during the Depression, London's economy remained steady, thanks to the demand for new consumer goods such as cars, electrical appliances and cheap furniture. After the Second World War, the Festival of Britain in 1951 was, like its predecessor a century before, a celebration of the country's manufacturing skills. Young designers like myself, who participated in the exhibition, confidently expected a huge surge of orders to result from the show, although it did not quite turn out like that. As late as 1961 London was still a major manufacturing centre, with 1.6 million workers employed in industries as varied as paper and printing, electronics, electrical engineering and clothing.

Change was swift and total. In little over a decade, London's industries all but vanished. Some 50,000 manufacturing jobs were lost every year in the period between 1961 and 1974 as factories closed and businesses moved out of the city. The reasons for this abrupt decline were various. Many factories and workshops were located in outdated premises, which made

Glass-blowing in L A Design studios in Camberwell, where glassware for the Conran shops and Conran Collection is made. The return of small craft makers to the city is an encouraging trend.

it difficult to expand and modernize. At the same time rental levels were too high to make the prospect of moving to a bigger city location economically feasible. Cheap imports from the Far East undercut locally made goods; poor transport made deliveries difficult. Once a few larger enterprises moved out of an area, the smaller businesses that remained found it difficult to survive.

By the early 1980s London's economy was increasingly based on the service industries: Mrs Thatcher appeared to hold the belief that the entire country could live on the strength of service industries alone. Computerization and e-commerce, and the deregulation of the financial markets – the City's Big Bang – have only accentuated this trend in recent years.

Nowadays London makes a great deal of money, but it no longer makes many things. I believe this is an unhealthy state of affairs for any city or society. Once, workshops and small factories were scattered around every London borough, on hinterland sites just a stone's throw from residential areas. Just as unhealthy as an overreliance on the service sector is a segregation of living and working. It is quite clear that the most successful communities in the long term are those of mixed use, where people live, work and enjoy themselves within the same relatively circumscribed area. The dead dormitory town or suburb, the featureless industrial park, the decaying inner city all come about when there is this relentless separation.

Underpinning it all is the value of land. During the boom years of the 1980s, as property values soared, millions of square feet of office space were built in London, much of it surplus to requirements. In some cases it paid developers to keep office blocks empty and gamble on the continuing escalation in rental levels. Then the bubble burst, the property market collapsed and recession set in.

One of the most conspicuous empty office blocks in London at the beginning of the recession was One Canada Square, the tower at Canary Wharf and the dominant feature of the Docklands development. Docklands was conceived originally as a new financial and commerical centre to rival the City. Here there was plenty of space to build the modern dealing rooms and offices that multinational companies required, provision that could not readily be accommodated within the City. Equally important, there was an urgent need to do something about the blight that had descended on the area since the old docks closed. In the 1980s 20,000 jobs were lost in Docklands.

Until that time the City had kept very tight control over new development within its confines, which served to keep rental levels high. It was difficult to get permission for a new

building and very difficult indeed to get permission for a tall building. All that changed as soon as the City looked over its shoulder and saw a potential new rival emerging in the east. Suddenly planning restrictions loosened with a vengeance. Nearly half of the City's office space was rebuilt during the 1980s.

The recession highlighted many of the anomalies of such speculative development. Next to the building at Shad Thames, where my design and architecture practice Conran & Partners is located, is a building that was first constructed as office space. The original developers fitted it out with all the features modern companies were thought to require – air-conditioning, automatic blinds, raised floors – at vast expense. Then came the recession. All the companies initially interested in taking the building rejected it because the costs of servicing and maintenance were so prohibitive. New developers then removed the air-conditioning, installed opening windows, took out all the false floors and put what had been originally designed as

Designed by Edward Cullinan and Robin Nicholson, the University of East London, located near the City of London Airport, promises to be a significant factor in the ongoing regeneration of Docklands. It is the first new university campus in the city for 50 years.

FAR RIGHT: Hussein Chalayan's 'skirtable', shown in the designer's Winter 2000 collection at Sadler's Wells theatre, was apparently inspired by the plight of refugees, whose possessions are necessarily reduced to those they can carry with them. It could equally symbolize the cross-fertilization of London's creative industries.

office space onto the market as luxury apartments. Similarly, in the City and other commercial areas of London, space that simply cannot be shifted as offices is increasingly being converted for residential use.

Docklands is only just beginning to come into its own. With the arrival of the Jubilee Line Extension there is an air of animation about the place that was entirely missing only a few years ago. The tower at Canary Wharf is now let and a sprinkling of restaurants are opening along the waterfront. When Tony Blair chose One Canada Square as the location for the French summit in 1999, the message was loud and clear: here is a forward-looking economy, not one mired in tradition and ritual. Conran & Partners was asked to come up with a scheme to design and fit out the meeting rooms with the best of contemporary British art and furniture and, in the brief ten days at our disposal, managed to create a setting that expressed this new commitment to creativity and modernity. It was all a far cry from the days, long ago, when we were engaged by Lord Gowrie, then Minister for the Arts under the Conservatives, to redesign his offices in Whitehall. The modernity of the interior came in for quite considerable flack, and was perceived as inappropriately 'luxurious', despite the fact that it actually cost considerably less than the usual ministerial refit, which more typically tended to feature hand-blocked wallpaper and an antique partner's desk, now rather bizarrely favoured by our Lord Chancellor.

Elsewhere in London, there are some small but very encouraging signs that work, in the old-fashioned hands-on sense, is also making something of a comeback. Craftspeople used automatically to make for the country to set up their studios. Now workshops are springing up all over London in cheap commercial or redundant industrial spaces – places such as Balls Pond Studios in Islington, Cockpit Arts in Holborn and 301½ Workshops in Vauxhall where people run small furniture-making businesses, throw

ABOVE: A porter shoulders a carcass in Smithfield meat market, one of the few wholesale markets in London still to trade from its original site.

pots, blow glass or produce any of the individually designed and made items that are increasingly attractive to consumers bored with the mediocre and mass-produced.

The archetypal cheap business space has always been the London railway arch. Until fairly recently, however, most railway-arch businesses were of the dodgy secondhand-car variety, where number plates were changed, mileages surreptitiously adjusted, and rust and dents given hasty spray jobs. Now there is an astonishing variety of enterprises: everything from patisseries to recording studios, upholsterers to health clubs.

There is also a renewed appreciation for London's surviving markets. Smithfield, which was once threatened with closure, has been restored to its multicoloured Victorian splendour and still echoes to the sound of meat porters hauling carcasses into cold storage. There are plans to develop Borough Market, the only fresh-food market in London that has traded from the same site for all of its 240-year history. Borough Market and its surrounding streets constitute one of London's true time warps. The gritty Dickensian atmosphere is so authentic that the area is in constant demand as a film location. The popular film *Lock, Stock and Two Smoking Barrels* was shot in the area. Instead of converting Borough Market into a sanitized tourist attraction – which, to my mind, has been the somewhat unfortunate fate of Covent Garden – the idea is to promote it as 'London's larder', a centre where suppliers and producers of high-quality food can market their wares. Such 'farmers' markets', including Islington's hugely successful Sunday-morning market, represent a new and very welcome development in city trading.

In a city founded on trade, markets have often served as the forcing ground for budding entrepreneurs. Camden Lock, where all of Europe's youth seems to descend at weekends, is a ragtag collection of stalls, junk shops, cafés and vans that sell every conceivable variety of fast food, all crammed into the streets around the canalside. It's messy and crowded but unmistakably alive: many successful retailers and designers have begun their careers with a pitch on the Lock.

Markets bring life back to street level, a buzz of activity that is the antithesis of the hermetically sealed world of the office block. Ever since the 1960s London has always gained creative inspiration from the street. Its creative industries – fashion, design, architecture, music, new media, film and graphics – are now seen to lead the world, and designers of international stature such as Philippe Starck are increasingly keen to work here. 'Cool Britannia' and all the associated hype over London's new status as the world capital of creativity has obscured what I consider to be a more important truth, however, which is that in terms of design and fashion London has been in the vanguard since the 1960s. The main difference between now and then is that our best and brightest talents used to have to leave the country to find commercial success. Now they more often stay put.

Unlike other countries in Europe or around the world, Britain has always trained vast numbers of artists and designers, even though there used to be few employment opportunities for such graduates. When I was a student at the Central School of Art and Design there were 33 others in my textile class, and hardly one subsequently found work in a related

area. Before I had completed the course, I was offered a job. Dora Batty, who ran the class, encouraged me to take it rather than stay and finish my degree – the opportunity was then so rare.

More than 20 years ago, when Mrs Thatcher was Minister for Education, I chaired a committee looking into the role of art and design in secondary education. I am glad to say that our recommendations – making the essential point that design should be integrated into the secondary-school curriculum – were accepted. Design is now the fourth most popular subject in secondary schools after maths, science and English, and the least truanted. The result is a generation of young people who are much more design-literate and more inclined to aspire to a job in one of the creative industries.

The rector of the Royal College of Art and new Chairman of the Design Council, Professor Christopher Frayling, maintains that London is now the world capital of design, with overseas students flocking to the city to experience its creative energy. He notes that what is new about design education is the move away from specialization towards an interweaving of different disciplines.

This new cross-fertilization can be detected in the work of many of London's talented young designers. A vivid illustration of the mind set could be seen at a recent London Fashion Week. Hussein Chalayan, Designer of the Year for two years running, produced a memorable show in which models peeled off soft covers from chairs and wore them like dresses. The transformation was complete when one model stepped into the hole in the middle of a 'coffee table' and hoisted it up to turn it into a vast wooden hooped skirt. In the same sort of way, London furniture and lighting designer Tom Dixon's famous Jack light is part sculpture, part design – in fact, part light, part seat – and entirely reflects Dixon's refusal to be pigeonholed. As design director of Habitat, Tom also displays another trend, which is an increased commercial awareness. It is no longer enough to produce innovative designs in tiny production runs: commercial success is just as important as critical acclaim. He has realized that to design and produce wonderfully creative work that is so expensive that it either fails to sell or ends up only in the homes of the very rich is a rather frustrating and undemocratic occupation.

Sir Peter Hall, an academic noted for his analyses of urban life and development, has said that 'the successful city is fizzing in some way intellectually'. Great cities, he argues – centres of power, money and exchange – embody the Establishment, but it is this very quality that attracts the outsiders and avant-garde who are keen to kick over the traces and spur the changes that keep places alive and full of vitality.

London has fizzed in the past, but the fizz has often gone flat rather rapidly. In the Swinging Sixties, when London gave the world the miniskirt, the Beatles topped the charts and photographers, hairdressers and models became style leaders, the impact of this revolutionary shift in lifestyle was actually limited – to a few London streets, a handful of people and a time frame of less than a decade. They say that if you can remember the Sixties, you weren't there. I was there – I opened my first Habitat shop in the Fulham Road in 1964 – and what I do remember is just what a small world it all was. Punk, the style that bubbled up from the street in the late 1970s, was even more short-lived. What is different about London's present creative blossoming is that for the first time it looks like having some staying power.

I feel quite optimistic when I realize the extent to which creativity is increasingly valued in Britain. London has always had its share of trade fairs, but until only a few years ago the success of a venture such as 100% Design would have been unthinkable. 100% Design, an annual event that showcases the best of contemporary design, is evidence of a profound sea change in the way we view the world in both its professionalism and its modernity. Unlike the numerous antiques fairs of London's events calendar, 100% Design champions the innovative and the cutting edge. Even the Ideal Home Exhibition is getting in on the act. Among the countless miracle kitchen gadgets on display there have been some inspirational new ideas featured in recent years. Rather than using accepted stylistic conventions they imagine houses of the future, not as a space-age fantasy, but as a real, achievable ideal.

Throughout my career, I have argued long and hard about the importance of design – not as an optional extra but rather as an integral part of industrial production. Previous governments did not precisely share this view: one has only to remember Mrs Thatcher ostentatiously draping her handkerchief over the tail of a model BA jet displaying the company's new corporate logo. Yet on the occasion of the Design Museum's tenth anniversary in October 1999 I was particularly heartened by a speech made by the Chancellor of the Exchequer, Gordon Brown. In a show of passionate support, he spelled out the government's commitment to design as a force for economic growth and a way of improving the quality of people's everyday lives. 'Economic success is not a product of luck,' he claimed, 'but of design.' If London is to maintain its present economic success, and become once again a place where things are made, design will have to play an even more critical role in the future.

Millions of people across the country wake up to the sound of *Today*, BBC Radio 4's morning news and current affairs programme. One of *Today*'s most distinctive presenters, John Humphrys, is shown here broadcasting *Wales on Sunday* from the BBC's central London studios.

The City's busiest terminal is Liverpool Street station, recently renovated and improved (ABOVE). Morning rush hour on London Bridge, with commuters pouring into the City (ABOVE RIGHT).

FAR LEFT: East London's most visible landmark is Cesar Pelli's One Canada Square, the tower that dwarfs the redevelopment of the area formerly occupied by the West India Docks. Initiated by Canadian developers Olympia and Yorke, the Canary Wharf complex is still very much under construction but has an increasing buzz as an increasing number of companies locate their businesses here.

LEFT: King's Bench Walk, Inner Temple. Some of the most graceful survivors of historic working London are the four Inns of Court – Lincoln's Inn, Middle Temple, Inner Temple and Gray's Inn – the traditional location of solicitors' offices and barristers' chambers. The Inns are thought to date from the fourteenth century.

Around 250,000 people work in the City, the 'Square Mile' that occupies roughly the same area as Roman and later medieval London. Nowhere in the capital are the layers of history piled up so thickly. Leadenhall Market, for example, stands on the site of the old Roman forum (FAR RIGHT). An elegant arcade built in 1881, Leadenhall's shops today purvey game, seafood and other delicacies to City workers. Similarly, the modern Stock Exchange, which provides all the technical facilities required for global trading, may only date from 1972, but there has been an Exchange on the same site since 1801 (TOP RIGHT). Many City workers, like these traders on the new international financial futures and options exchange, are in the business of making money out of money (CENTRE RIGHT). Watching indoor football at Spitalfields Market provides a little light relief during lunch breaks (BELOW RIGHT).

Essential services: nurse on duty at Great Ormond Street Children's Hospital (ABOVE); the busy Accident and Emergency department at the Royal London Hospital on Whitechapel Road (TOP RIGHT); police motorcyclists in Mayfair (BOTTOM RIGHT).

OVERLEAF: **Furniture designer Greg James' studio is a house on stilts near Brick Lane, once the control room for a locomotive watertower.**

BRASSERI

The works canteen is an enshrined part of office culture. For London's cabbies, the equivalent is the
cab shelter which supplies simple fare, endless cups of tea and companionship in the breaks between
ferrying passengers around the capital (ABOVE). In a recent comparative study between different
navigational aids, a black-cab driver, armed with the 'Knowledge', beat electronic gadgets hands down.
A rather more rarefied atmosphere is displayed by the canteen at the riverside offices of Foster and
Partners (RIGHT).

PREVIOUS PAGES: Construction workers have a meeting – or a tea break? (LEFT). Kitchen staff at Soho Brasserie take a breather (RIGHT).

The working day at Billingsgate, one of the world's greatest wholesale fish markets, begins before dawn as lorries arrive with crates of every imaginable sort of fish packed in ice, ready for sale to fishmongers and restaurateurs.

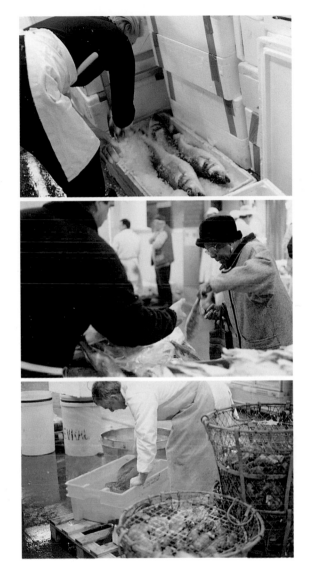

Keeping people amused is a serious business. Circus Space in Hoxton, east
London is the country's premier training centre for acrobats and aerialists
(LEFT). Holy Trinity Church in Dalston is the setting for the annual celebration of
the life of Joseph Grimaldi, a service which takes place on the second Sunday in
February and is attended by clowns from around the world in full 'slap' (ABOVE).
Grimaldi, one of London's most famous clowns, was born in Islington and gave
his farewell performance in 1828.

London Fashion Week draws buyers and media attention from around the world to
view the work of designers such as Boudicca (LEFT) and Alexander McQueen, whose
2000 show took place at Gainsborough Studios, where Hitchcock once filmed (ABOVE).

These London jobs fall squarely into the category 'someone's-got-to-do-it': washing the clockface of **Big Ben** (right); dusting off the bronze figures of the **Horseguards Memorial** (ABOVE LEFT); touching up **Guardsmen's webbing** (ABOVE RIGHT); and painting white lines on one of the runways at **Heathrow Airport** (LEFT).

PREVIOUS PAGES: Tinker, tailor, soldier ... blacksmith, puppet-maker. Blacksmith David Townsend in his Hammersmith forge (LEFT); Jan Zalud, puppet-maker for the Little Angel Theatre, Islington (RIGHT).

Kentish Town is a rather unlikely setting for the office of an e-commerce company, but then again an office is a rather unlikely setting for a lawn (ABOVE). Design company Nowicka Stern has provided an unusual meeting space for another.com, a business that supplies personalized e-mail addresses. The lawn is watered from underneath; ultraviolet light provides daylight conditions. Brick Lane is fast becoming a centre for other e-businesses and creative industries. Here a film crew sets up on location at the Truman Brewery (LEFT).

OVERLEAF: The Biomedical Sciences building at Imperial College, designed by Foster and Partners.

Shopping

When Napoleon described England as a nation of shopkeepers it was presumably intended as an insult. The negative implications of the remark are fairly obvious – shopkeeping was the ultimate petit-bourgeois occupation. By extension, a nation of shopkeepers could only be a sedentary, cautious and insular people – hardly worth invading.

There is little evidence of such insularity among London retailers today. If you shop in London, you shop around the world. Contemporary London is a bazaar of global retailing: saris in Southall, Brick Lane and Green Street; Chinese bric-a-brac in Soho; and exotic imports from just about any place on the planet on sale in markets and shops across the capital. In addition, every major international retailer has at least one outlet in the city; many of these companies view London and Manhattan as retail locations of equal importance.

This cultural diversity is matched by an equally stimulating blend of the traditional and the cutting edge. There are emporia and quirky specialist shops, chic designer stores and flea markets, shops that undergo a facelift and refit every other season and those that have remained more or less unchanged for centuries. I cannot think of a better city in the world for indulging in a little retail therapy.

Shopping is the favourite pastime of many Londoners and one of the capital's biggest draws. While London is not quite 'the city that never sleeps', longer opening hours and Sunday trading have transformed the city's image. When I look back on my Hampstead childhood, I remember weekends as endless stretches of boredom. Nothing ever seemed to happen: the image that always springs to mind when I think of those days is Walter Sickert's *Ennui*. Today, Hampstead heaves with people every Saturday and Sunday and most of them, when they are not eating or drinking, are shopping.

For those who are keen on tradition, London, a city that was founded on trade, has a great commercial heritage. The oldest shops in London date back two or three hundred years. Fortnum & Mason was founded in 1707; the wine merchants Berry Bros & Rudd predate it by nine years. Hamley's began life in 1760 as Noah's Ark, a toy shop in Holborn where William Hamley sold tin soldiers and rocking horses. Many retail survivors from London's past are small specialist shops, producing and selling bespoke goods. There are the hatmakers James Lock & Co, the shoemakers John Lobb and, one of my favourites, Tanner Krolle, which

LEFT: 'Classics with a twist' – such as this women's suit patterned with the A–Z, the London street map – are the stock-in-trade of British designer Paul Smith.

ABOVE: Fortnum & Mason on Piccadilly, purveyor of fine foods and delicacies since the early eighteenth century, is famous for its sumptuous displays and tail-coated sales assistants.

London abounds in specialist shops. The Hive in south London sells a wide range of different types of honey and also features a wall of live bees.

produces exceptionally fine leather luggage. Enter one of these shops and you are entering a lost world, where everything is handmade to individual specification, no matter how eccentric. You are also privy to the arcane knowledge of the specialist purveyor; Fortnum's, apparently, can advise on which particular tea suits your drinking water (you provide the sample). The encyclopaedic mind of the antiquarian book dealer is equally impressive. I treasure a book of steel engravings of the Eiffel Tower that dealer David Batterham managed to unearth, as if by magic, from the delightful chaos of his shop.

The specialist shop appeals to our sense of continuity and flatters our powers of discrimination – even if, at times, it can be hard on the wallet. Such shops also offer the sheer delight that is felt when every conceivable variation on a theme is on display. James Smith & Sons, whose glazed shopfront is a Victorian remnant amid the modern mediocrity of New Oxford Street, sells nothing but umbrellas and walking sticks. One of the newer specialist shops I particularly enjoy is V.V. Rouleaux, a treasure trove of ribbons, trimmings and all forms of passementerie; while John Sandoe, near Sloane Square, is my idea of a perfect bookshop.

At the opposite end of the shopping spectrum is the all-inclusive department store. The department store is not a home-grown phenomenon and was late to arrive in London. Bon Marché in Paris – described by Zola as a 'cathedral of commerce' – had already been established for 20 years when London's first department stores opened their doors.

The precursor of the department store in London was the arcade, a covered lane that provided an all-weather enclosure for a variety of independent specialist shops; the elegant Burlington Arcade, which dates from Regency times, is one of the few remaining examples. Early London department stores, which started appearing around the 1880s, were rather similar in form and consisted of clusters of shops offering a range of goods and services, but under single management. The very first was Whiteley's in Bayswater, which grew to 160 departments and styled itself as a 'universal provider'. Harrods, perhaps the world's most famous department store, followed soon after. The present building, a grand terracotta edifice, dates from 1901–5.

The location of Harrods in Knightsbridge was symptomatic of the shift of London's main shopping district from the environs of the City to Oxford Street, Regent Street, Piccadilly and points west. By Edwardian times stores such as Debenham & Freebody, Marshall & Snelgrove and Swan & Edgar were catering for a new type of shopper, providing a respectable haven where middle-class women could browse, take tea and make a few purchases. Increasingly such stores were no longer groups of related shops but were purpose-built, with all the latest in technological features. In 1898 Harrods was the first department store to install an escalator; at its inauguration a Harrods assistant was stationed at the top, armed with sal volatile and brandy for those whose nerves were not quite up to the thrills of the 'moving staircase'.

Harrods still provides, under a single roof, a range of goods and services that is almost dotty in its comprehensiveness, a vast scope that is more than enough to merit its nineteenth-century claim 'Harrods serves the world'. One million square feet of retail space are arranged over its seven floors. Of particular appeal for the thousands of tourists who visit every year are the spectacular tiled Edwardian food halls. Then there are fashion and designer wear, shoes,

hats, accessories, perfume, cosmetics and everything else you expect in a major West End store. But you can also have your umbrella repaired or your hair barbered, book theatre tickets, change foreign currency, arrange a holiday, or even buy a house at the in-store estate agency; the undertaking service has, however, been discontinued. The music-hall comedienne Bea Lillie once bought an alligator in the Harrods pet store to give to Noël Coward as a Christmas present.

Harrods gained a major rival in 1909 with the opening of Selfridges on Oxford Street, founded by Gordon Selfridge, the famous American retailer. He had previously been associated with the hugely successful Chicago store Marshall Field, and introduced

a new approach to retailing, with a greater emphasis on stylish presentation and attractive window displays to entice customers inside. The new store was exceptionally smart for its day; it was also enormous, occupying an entire block. The main Oxford Street entrance, marked by a clock featuring an 11-foot figure, *The Queen of Time*, became a popular meeting place.

The original scheme for the building, designed by a Chicago architect, also included an immense tower, but this was never built. It is interesting that this idea has now resurfaced in a new proposal put forward by Selfridges to develop an area to the rear of the store; the plan is to create a tower with restaurants and bars offering panoramic views of the city.

Window-shopping meets sculpture in *Autumn Intrusion*, an installation for Harvey Nichols by Thomas Heatherwick.

Selfridges, so revolutionary for its time, has suffered somewhat in recent years, like many other department stores. Harrods is secure in its role as one of London's must-see sights (although few Londoners still regard it as their store). Harvey Nichols, with its smart restaurant, innovative window displays and up-to-the-minute fashion department, has carved out a niche as the haunt of those formidable 'ladies who lunch' – its role in the BBC's *Absolutely Fabulous*, as the favourite shop of those fictional fashionistas, Patsy and Edina, has done its image absolutely no harm. Other stores have struggled rather harder to keep up. Selfridges' response to a dwindling market share has been a style makeover, masterminded by its new director Vittorio Radice, formerly director of Habitat. A glamorous revamped interior, together with a wide range of new places to eat in dotted around the store, has begun to win back customers, laying the foundations for what I believe will be future success.

At the Conran Shop we use imaginative displays, themed groupings of products and room sets to guide and inspire the customer.

The slow eclipse of the department store actually dates back to the 1960s, when it was challenged on two fronts. The first was the emergence of the 'boutique' with its rapid turnover of high fashion at cheap prices. The second was the arrival of the 'lifestyle' store.

When I was a young furniture designer starting out in the 1950s, many department stores and large furniture outlets served as warehouses for goods produced by other firms. There was little attempt to display the stock in an attractive way; it was simply all jumbled together on grey counters lit by fluorescent light. Furthermore, a purchase offered no instant gratification whatsoever and customers often had to wait many weeks for delivery.

My instincts told me that the time was now right for a new type of shop selling furniture and household goods to a young, and more open-minded clientele. Habitat was a huge gamble, but when the first shop opened in the Fulham Road in 1964 it was an immediate critical success.

Habitat's core merchandise was flat-pack furniture. I predicted, correctly as it turned out, that the minor inconvenience of self-assembly would be massively outweighed by the immediate pleasure of taking purchases home on the spot. (Our byline was 'Habitat for that can't wait to get it home feeling'.) The shop looked different, too. Instead of the rather dull, suburban atmosphere of the average furniture department in the average department store, our goods were arranged in room sets that suggested ways in which they could be put together at home: we were selling not merely individual products, but a whole new way of living.

Most people, however, do not make major furniture purchases very often – there is a limit to how many kitchen tables or beds one is going to need. To keep customers coming back, and to reinforce the lifestyle quality of the shop, we also stocked a wide range of smaller household goods – everything from tea towels and cushions to garlic presses, casseroles and chicken bricks – which our team of buyers sourced from around the world. These were arranged not in room sets but stacked high in thematic groups to give an impression of generosity and visual plenitude. It was radical, and it worked. I expected Habitat to be only ever a single shop; eventually it grew to be a big chain, with many international outlets.

Habitat was one of a new breed of design-led retailers such as Biba, Mary Quant, Foale & Tuffin and Ossie Clarke, whose cumulative effect, together with Carnaby Street, had a major impact on the perception of London as a modern shopping city – an impact somewhat out of proportion to the actual size of the businesses concerned. These early 'lifestyle' stores also marked the beginning of the trend for retailers themselves to become brands, a phenomenon that defined the modern British high street in the 1980s. In a traditional department store dozens of brands compete for the customer's attention. Where the retailer itself is the brand, the act of selection is implicit when the customer enters the store. The arrival in London of global brands, such as the hugely successful Gap, has not only brought increasing competition for home-grown chains, but also altered expectations and shopping patterns.

London is an important location for major international labels. Prada spells out its exclusivity with bouncers on the door at the Old Bond Street branch.

Design – everything from signage to packaging to the retail interior – has increasingly been used to reinforce such brand identities, with leading architects such as David Chipperfield, John Pawson, Rashied Din and Eva Jiricna drafted in to create stores that are as much architectural *tours de force* as they are places in which to buy things. This is not, of course, solely a feature of London or even British retailing, but the result has been far more sophisticated retail environments and far more discriminating consumers. Consider the current difficulties experienced by a long-established retailer such as Marks & Spencer; unimaginative presentation of stock and dreary shop interiors may not be all that ails the chain but formerly loyal customers are no longer prepared to overlook them.

Service has seen a similar shake-up. The *Are You Being Served?* stereotype of British retailing, as immortalized in the department-store sitcom – part condescension, part indifference and a large part incompetence – has not entirely disappeared but is being increasingly challenged

**Paul Smith's shop in Notting Hill
trades on the homey setting, with
clothing, accessories and furnishings
displayed over several floors of a
terraced house.**

by what might be seen as a North American approach of meeting the customer more than halfway. In this context, the mobility of labour brought about by Britain's membership of the EU has also had an effect; so, too, has the relaxation of restrictions on Sunday trading.

In the 1980s government took some persuading that shopping on Sundays was appropriate. Lifestyles had changed and in many families both adults worked full time; it seemed particularly anomalous for shops to open only during normal working hours and remain closed on the one day when people had time off. As chairman of 'Open Shop' I did my best to present the case. When a bill to deregularize shop-opening hours eventually came before Parliament, it faced stiff opposition from many large and traditional retailers, the Church and butchers. I was dispatched to see Mrs Thatcher to gain her support, a task I approached with some trepidation.

To my surprise the Prime Minister started to reminisce about her father, a highly religious man who had been a grocer in Grantham. She recalled that during the Second World War he had been concerned about the young servicemen wandering around the streets on Sundays with nothing to do, and how he had wanted to open his shop for them.

Although Mrs Thatcher became a convert to the cause of Sunday opening, the bill was defeated, largely owing to the efforts of the Ulster Unionists who wished to discomfit the Prime Minister at that particular moment. Several years later, however, it was passed. Today, Sunday almost equals Saturday as the best day for sales, and the flexibility of opening hours has added immeasurably to the convenience and pleasure of London shopping.

With the rise of lifestyle shopping there has been an increasing convergence of market sectors that used to be quite distinct. Every fashion designer now has to have a range of homewares, together with an in-store café or restaurant. When French-born Nicole Farhi opened her Bond Street shop it included Nicole's, a restaurant; now there is a separate shop selling furniture and furnishings. One of fashion designer Paul Smith's latest ventures is a shop arranged over several floors of a terraced house in Notting Hill. The bulk of the stock remains clothing, principally menswear, but there are also furnishings and toys for sale: the point is the homey setting. There is a new florist's shop in the City that doubles as a café – or is it a café that sells flowers? The inclusivity of such shops turns them into destinations in themselves.

As far as destination is concerned, entrepreneurial retailing can change an area very quickly. The rental values are so high in smart shopping areas such as Bond Street that only major retailers or brands can now afford to be located there. In any event, it is unlikely that a flagship store on Bond Street or Sloane Street will make any money; its purpose is to provide a commercial presence or showcase, a cheaper form of promotion than advertising. Nike Town, for example, at its prominent Oxford Circus site, is more about brand positioning than shifting stock. For up-and-coming retailers the answer is often to pick a location that is marginally off the beaten track and hope to make a success of it.

Brick Lane was certainly off the beaten track a few years ago. Situated to the east of Shoreditch, this desperately deprived area has seen successive waves of immigrants arrive ever since the Huguenots settled here, fleeing religious persecution in seventeenth-century France. After the Huguenots came Jewish refugees from Europe, who were followed by Bengali immigrants, resulting in a cultural mix that explains Brick Lane's proliferation of curry houses and sweatshops serving the rag trade. Brick Lane is also the home of a street market renowned equally for its vibrancy and the impoverished nature of some of its wares.

Brick Lane is dominated by the ten-acre site of the old Truman Brewery, whose empty buildings have recently provided an irresistible attraction for those seeking cheap commercial space; the increasing concentration of new-media companies has earned Brick Lane the nickname 'Silicon Alley'. Workshops, studios and shops have sprung up, from Atlantis, the largest art-supply shop in London, to shops selling the latest in contemporary design. A branch of the Japanese-owned World Design Laboratory has opened here; its tunnel-like entrance, complete with stepping stones and macabre artefacts, is not for the faint-hearted. A similar message is spelled out by a neighbouring shop selling contemporary design classics, provocatively called Eat My Handbag Bitch. At a recent opening of an exhibition featuring work donated by various London artists in aid of a children's charity, I was somewhat amused by the sight of limousines queuing up outside the Truman Brewery to drop off their fashionably dressed stiletto-heeled passengers, people who no doubt would never have dreamed of setting foot in this part of the city only a few years ago.

Marylebone High Street was not quite the same sort of outpost as Brick Lane when, several years ago, we acquired a site at the top end of the street, but it had never really recovered from the recession. Our new Conran Shop and restaurant, Orrery, located in a building that was once a stable, has kick-started a process of regeneration in the surrounding area.

At Bluebird in the King's Road, we set out to create a 'gastrodrome', combining restaurants, bars, a café and a member's club with a foodstore and forecourt market.

Similarly, Conduit Street, off Regent Street, where we opened our first Conran Collection shop, has been radically transformed, seemingly overnight, from the rather nondescript location of airline offices to an alternative Bond Street, where designers such as Vivienne Westwood, Joseph, Issey Miyake and Alexander McQueen have recently opened new stores. As was the case for Marylebone High Street, the spur was provided by low rents and empty shops, together with a location that had been almost ludicrously overlooked, given its centrality. Rents will certainly now rise.

One black cloud currently hovering over the heads of London retailers, however, is the rise in e-commerce. Most shops operate with quite low margins and even a slight drop in sales can spell collapse due to unprofitability. The risk is greater for shops selling other people's brands and for those selling products that are inherently e-commerceable, such as books, for example. If shopping on the Net becomes more popular, I fear we may see London shops fail in quantities, or at least those whose products are bland and commonplace and therefore Netable.

The silver lining in the black cloud may well be the return of small specialist shops offering both high-quality goods and produce and high standards of face-to-face personal service – the latter being something that the Net, however interactive, simply cannot offer. I can remember when the King's Road was a true village high street, lined with greengrocers, butchers and bakers. Internet shopping, ironically, may encourage a revival of this much-missed shopping pattern. Many people welcome the opportunity to shop on line when it relieves them of the drudgery of the weekly trip to the supermarket. After all, it is simply not necessary to buy certain predictable household staples in person, and it is a great deal better for our traffic-clogged streets if a single delivery van can take the place of many individual shoppers driving to and from superstores. But there are equally many types of purchase that cannot be made virtually, and whose selection offers more inherent pleasures. One might well be prepared to order a month's supply of loo rolls on line, but would we really be happy to forego the trip to the delicatessen, with its appetizing aromas, choose a sofa without sitting on it or buy a dress without trying it on? E-commerce could have the potential to free people for the type of shopping they truly enjoy.

When I was setting up Habitat one of my inspirations was the ordinary street markets that you find in any French town of significant size. The directness and sensuousness of markets still appeal to me powerfully. Ordinary basic items, which would look rather forlorn on their own, acquire an almost sculptural quality en masse, while the colours, scents and textures of fresh produce mount an agreeable assault on the senses. The sheer animation of competing stallholders and bargaining customers is a far cry from the torpid supermarket aisle.

London's wholesale markets have had a rather chequered history. Smithfield has managed to hang on, despite repeated attempts by residents of the surrounding area to have it closed down. The architectural fabric of Covent Garden was preserved when the old fruit and flower market departed in 1974, but the conservationists' victory has proved rather hollow as the area has become more and more of a trite tourist attraction. Spitalfields, on the eastern fringe of the City, also faces redevelopment but in the interim it offers a delightfully quirky combination of stalls selling organic produce, eccentric interiors shops, ethnic cafés and small restaurants.

London's flea markets have proved somewhat more resilient. Portobello Road, perhaps the most famous of them all, manages to retain something of its original flavour, particularly at its northern end. Bermondsey in southeast London is still the place to go on Friday mornings if you are looking for antique or secondhand furniture; it is also the place to scour, it is rumoured, if you are looking for one of your own antiques that has been stolen! Alfie's Antique Market in Church Street, Marylebone has over 200 dealers specializing in various period and retro styles, while another cluster of dealers and junk shops can be found in the lanes of Camden Passage, Islington and in the nearby Mall, a converted tram shed. Like the capital's many auction houses and architectural-salvage yards, the persistence of such markets is proof of a passion for recycling the past in a contemporary context.

What I find perhaps more surprising and heartening is the survival of the ordinary London street market. After the Great Fire, attempts were made to shift trading – along with its attendant congestion, crime and disorder – off the city streets, but the street market never entirely disappeared. Away from the centre of London, every area still seems to have one, selling fruit and veg, household sundries, sometimes fish, sometimes cheap clothing, together with a couple of stalls selling goods of dodgy provenance and even more dubious quality. If you take a stroll down Ridley Road in Dalston, said to have been the inspiration for Walford market in the BBC's long-running soap *EastEnders*, there is a staggering variety of goods and produce on sale: dried salt cod and wet fish, wigs and hairpieces, halal meat, whole chickens and pigs' ears, huge bunches of fresh coriander and flat-leaf parsley, underwear to suit all sizes and shapes and sexes, luggage, bootleg videos and cassettes, Turkish sweets, African vegetables and Indian spices, spangly bracelets and bric-a-brac, pots and pans, binbags and bins …. A form of trading that is as old as the city itself, the street market is London shopping at its most direct and robust.

OVERLEAF: When Selfridges had to clean their building, they commissioned artist Sam Taylor-Wood to come up with something rather more interesting than the usual hoarding. The result was *XV Seconds*, a 900-foot-long frieze depicting 21 pop and cultural icons, a tongue-in-cheek reference to the Elgin Marbles.

London's many bespoke or specialist shops, which contribute so much to the pleasure of shopping in the city, are like delightful packages in themselves. In a shop that sells variations on a single theme, the customer's sense of discrimination is flattered; the bonus is often sales staff who are passionate about their products and know what they are talking about.

For dedicated window-shoppers, London's retailers provide a wealth of
street-level spectacle, often enlivened by a sense of irreverence and humour.
The subtle wit and implied tactility of Nina A's window-dressing in Brompton
Street is guaranteed to snag the attention of passers-by (RIGHT). Tiffany's
whimsical display is appropriately scaled for the jewellery it advertises, the tight
frame inviting close inspection (ABOVE).

Brick Lane, in the heart of the East End, has seen successive waves of immigrants settle here ever since the Huguenots arrived in the seventeenth century, the most recent being the Bangladeshis (LEFT). In the past few years, the vibrant street market, curry houses and outlets selling exotic textiles (BELOW) have been joined by cutting-edge design offices, internet companies and other young entrepreneurs attracted by cheap rents and the generous space offered by sites such as the former Truman Brewery (RIGHT AND BELOW RIGHT).

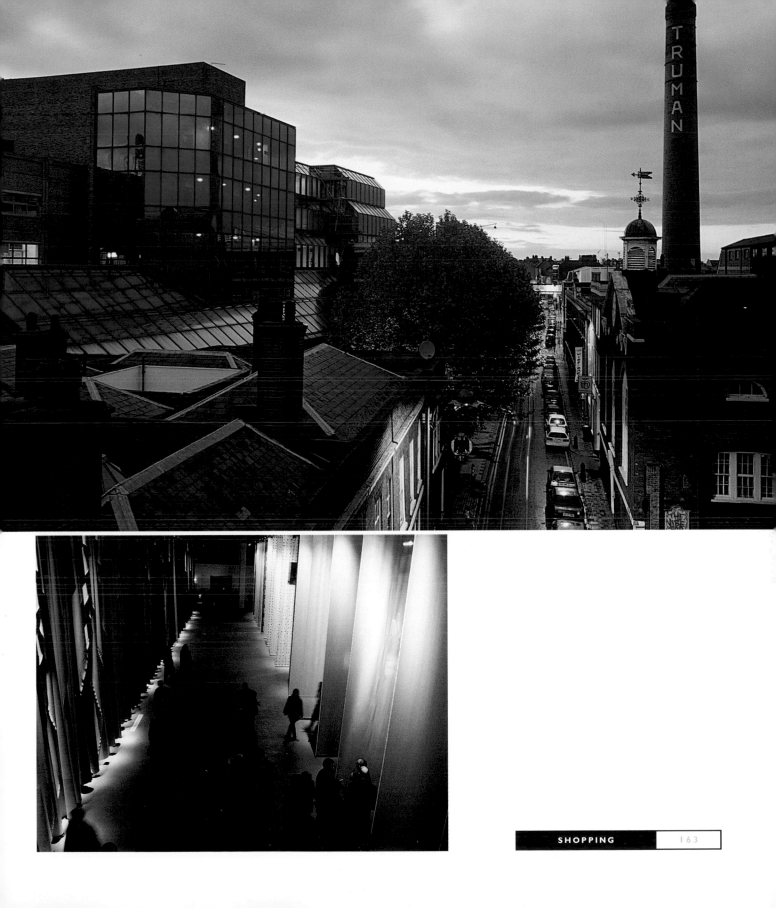

Architect-designed shop interiors provide a powerful means of reinforcing brand identity and, incidentally, parting shoppers from their cash. Minimalist John Pawson was drafted in by the fashion chain Jigsaw to create the elegantly spare interior of their New Bond Street branch (ABOVE). The Stussy store in Earlham Street, Covent Garden, sells clothing for skateboarding enthusiasts, its sloping planes of plywood evoking the activity itself (RIGHT).

OVERLEAF: In-store displays frame objects of desire at Lulu Guinness's shop (LEFT) and Alexander McQueen's Conduit Street shop (RIGHT).

Ever since the first department stores opened, with their tearooms and restaurants, eating and shopping have been natural companions. In recent years, however, the trend has accelerated. The fact that you can snack at **Books for Cooks** is perhaps not surprising; **Flowercity**, a florist's-cum-café, represents a more unusual pairing (FAR LEFT). **Harvey Nichols**, with its branch of **Yo! Sushi** (LEFT), restaurant and food market, makes the most of the connection. The basement restaurant, **Nicole's**, at the Bond Street Nicole Farhi shop, provides an ideal venue for ladies who lunch (ABOVE).

London's food markets, such as the bustling Berwick Street market, whet the appetite and provide plenty of opportunities to spot the eccentric punctuation of the 'greengrocer's apostrophe' (LEFT). A growing and thoroughly laudable trend has been the popularity of farmers' markets where specialist producers sell their wares. My son's eponymous shop, Tom's Deli in Notting Hill, is evidence of the revival of speciality food shops and delicatessens (ABOVE LEFT); while the exotic produce on sale in local markets reflects the multicultural mix of areas such as Brixton (ABOVE RIGHT).

Mystery and restraint can be as enticing as blatant display when attracting passing trade. A discreet sign announces the presence of Egg in Kinnerton Street, SW1, a delightful shop that sells contemporary craft and clothing (ABOVE LEFT). Egg's founder/owner Maureen Doherty used to work for Issey Miyake. Japanese chain Muji, famous for its 'no brand goods', has had a particular success in London (ABOVE RIGHT). Another Japanese import, World Design Laboratory near Brick Lane, features an entrance that is not for the faint-hearted, complete with stepping stones, traces of mummified hands and heads and a wailing soundtrack (RIGHT).

London's flea markets provide happy hunting grounds for urban treasure-seekers. Places to go include Spitalfields (LEFT), Portobello Road (CENTRE TOP), Bermondsey (CENTRE BOTTOM) and Greenwich (FAR RIGHT).

Precursors of department stores, London's few remaining arcades preserve the gentility and refinement of a previous age. The graceful Burlington Arcade in Piccadilly (RIGHT) was designed in 1819. A similar feeling for quality pervades Daunt Books on Marylebone High Street, a bookshop specializing in travel (BELOW). Curiosities, such as James Smith & Sons, the umbrella shop in Holborn that has been trading since 1857, miraculously manage to hold their own in face of rising rents and chain-store competition (FAR RIGHT).

OVERLEAF: The gaudy glamour of Oxford Street comes into its own when showbiz personalities switch on the Christmas lights. In 1999, it was the turn of Ronan Keating, lead singer with Boyzone.

There's rarely any snow and the January sales usually start in December, but the festive season provides an excuse for retailers to pile on the glitter. Harrods decks itself out with Christmas trees to add to the lights that cascade down its façade like so many strings of pearls (LEFT AND BELOW LEFT); while exclusive Bond Street shops transform themselves into elegant winter wonderlands (ABOVE AND ABOVE RIGHT). Window displays of sparkling mannequins stretch the boundaries of taste (BELOW RIGHT).

Eating and Drinking

It is safe to say that most people visiting London 15 or 20 years ago would have rated food fairly low down on the list of the city's attractions. In fact, you could probably say that food was a reason for not visiting London. Only the very well-heeled, eating at the best restaurants, could have expected positively to enjoy what was on offer in the capital; for everyone else it was largely a case of putting up with it. Today the breadth and excellence of London's restaurants are among the more remarkable and perhaps least expected changes to have occurred in the city.

Unlike many of the other transformations London has undergone recently, this dramatic improvement has been widely and publicly recognized. Along with New York, London is now acknowledged as a world leader in terms of the quality and quantity of its cuisine, setting trends in food and drink that others then proceed to copy. The vibrancy of its new restaurants, bars, hotels and clubs is the most visible sign of what amounts to a major cultural shift.

It is all a far cry from the situation at the end of the Second World War, when London had an entirely warranted reputation as a gastronomic desert. There were a few very expensive restaurants serving *haute cuisine*, with menus written entirely in French; there were cafés, including the admirably democratic Joe Lyons corner houses; fish and chip shops; eel, pie and mash shops; and a smattering of ethnic restaurants and sandwich bars – and very little in between. For young people like myself, only pubs offered the prospect of a social evening one could afford. Although the traditional London pub inspires fond memories, as I remember them, the aroma of stale sweat and beer and the fug of cigarette smoke are, like the monstrous hangovers I used to get after an evening drinking cheap cider at my local, best forgotten.

My first experience of going to a restaurant as a bill-paying adult was also one of my most embarrassing. My father had given me what was then the princely sum of 25 guineas to celebrate my 21st birthday in style. I invited seven friends to the Café de Paris, a restaurant-cum-nightspot famous for having taken a direct hit during the Blitz. We dined from the table d'hôte, drank a modest two bottles of wine, danced a little and all in all had a very jolly time. Until I asked for the bill, which came to £28.10s. It was with some mortification that I had to ask my friends to chip in – the only alternative was to do the washing-up!

The Cow in Westbourne Park Road has attracted a devoted following for its fresh seafood and traditional Irish pub atmosphere.

My Café de Paris birthday was an exception. Generally my friends and I cooked and ate at home. The sculptor Eduardo Paolozzi, whom I had met at art college, was keen on cooking, and through his family connections – the Paolozzis had an ice-cream business in Edinburgh – could always manage to get his hands on what were some very exotic ingredients for the time. One of the dishes to which he introduced me was Risotto Nero, conjured up from little tins of squid in their ink.

The dearth of good, affordable places to eat at in postwar London was symptomatic of the way that restaurants and hotels had developed. Unlike New York, Paris or other European cities, where restaurants were established early in the nineteenth century, it was not until nearly a century later that London could boast more than a handful. One reason for this was the success of the gentleman's club. Professional men could not only eat, drink and socialize at their clubs, they could also stay overnight in reasonably comfortable surroundings. The club was itself an evolution of the old coffee house, which had provided an informal meeting place for like-minded well-to-do men in the days when coffee was heavily taxed and therefore a drink for the elite. Aside from clubs, London did have other places to eat at, such as chop houses and taverns, but these, too, were exclusively male. For the working population, street sellers peddling eels and pies, whelks, oysters and fried fish supplemented pub fare.

The first true London restaurants appeared in the middle of the nineteenth century. A number, like the Café Royal and the Criterion, were associated with theatres, which, in its way, is not surprising when you consider what a theatrical experience eating out can be. The Café Royal, which was opened by a Parisian wine merchant in 1865, was glamorously and dramatically decorated with marble-topped tables and red-velvet seats, and became a fashionable artistic Edwardian haunt, favoured by Whistler, Oscar Wilde and Augustus John.

The next wave of London restaurants was associated with the grand hotels that began to emerge at the end of the century. The Savoy, perhaps the grandest of them all, was launched by Richard D'Oyly Carte, the great Victorian impresario who had made a fortune staging Gilbert and Sullivan operettas. The hotel, which opened in 1889, adjoined another D'Oyly Carte venture, the Savoy theatre, and was fitted out and furnished to a standard hitherto unknown in London, with a high proportion of bathrooms, as well as electric lights and electric lifts.

The Savoy's first manager was César Ritz, while Auguste Escoffier, who at that time was the most famous chef in the world, was in charge of the kitchens. The hotel built up a reputation for both excellence and service, taking pains to indulge the most eccentric whims of its rich and well-connected customers. Most importantly, the Savoy started a fashion for mixed-company dining, which was a trend that other hotel restaurants were then quick to exploit.

Despite the restaurant's increasing success as a venue where the wealthy could live the high life, there remained little for the ordinary middle-class Londoner until after the war. But it is probably fair to say that there was also little demand. With its connotations of luxury, a restaurant meal was still a rare indulgence, a treat that average people awarded themselves, their loved ones or their family on the occasion of some significant rite of passage: an engagement, a wedding anniversary or a new job, for example. Restaurant-going was simply not an entrenched part of most people's social lives.

All this began to change in the early 1950s, when Elizabeth David published her first books, distilling her experience of good provincial French and Mediterranean cooking. It was like a breath of fresh air – or air headily scented with the pungent aromas of garlic, olive oil and fresh thyme. The robust flavours of country cooking described on those pages made a striking contrast to the elaborate confections of traditional *haute cuisine*, which until then had been the extent of most people's understanding of foreign cookery. Elizabeth David's elegant prose, evoking the unpretentious charms of local bistros, cafés and restaurants or the sensuous pleasures of the ordinary Mediterranean food market, served to intellectualize the whole subject of food. Small restaurants owned and run by her disciples began to spring up in London; slowly and surely the tide began to turn.

Many of the new restaurants modelled themselves on the neighbourhood bistro, which in France was more often than not family run. The cosy informality of this style of eating out was not entirely unknown in London; the bohemian quarters of Soho and Fitzrovia had been the locations of a few family-run Italian restaurants before the war. Bertorelli's in Charlotte Street was founded by four Italian brothers in 1912 and was one of my favourite restaurants in the early days of my furniture and design business. Bianchi's in Frith Street, with its simple tiled interior, was run by the formidable Elena who went on to manage the rather grander L'Escargot and subsequently L'Etoile in Charlotte Street. The White Tower was another rather bohemian haunt in Charlotte Street; it was said that the private rooms above the restaurant were often rented out for illicit assignations. In the early days of my design business we rented one of them for a more sober purpose, to make a corporate-identity presentation to Harvey's of Bristol the sherry importers, and I am sure the choice of venue helped us win the job.

In addition to its trattoria, London also had a long-established Chinatown. At the beginning of each school term my mother would always take me to a Chinese restaurant near Piccadilly Circus before packing me off on the train. Like the homely Italian places, one of the attractions of Chinese restaurants was their inexpensiveness. But however affordable the meals, such exotic cooking remained a minority enthusiasm, good for an excursion once in a while, but far from a mainstream or fashionable choice. Then, in the 1960s, two restaurants opened that challenged people's perceptions of, for the want of a better term, the 'ethnic' restaurant. Terrazzo in Soho, an Italian restaurant run by Mario and Franco, was the epitome of chic and an extremely fashionable spot. A similar shock of the new was provided by Michael Chow's Chinese restaurant in Kensington, Mr Chow, with its Italian waiters and contemporary interior. The architect Rick Mather's 1980s makeover of the Zen chain of Chinese restaurants is a more recent example of the same approach.

Today you can eat your way around the world without actually leaving London. The aromatic flavours of Vietnamese cuisine can be sampled at the unpretentious Viet Hoa in Hackney.

Today, London's cultural diversity is reflected in the huge range of different styles of cooking on offer in the capital's burgeoning number of restaurants: from Vietnamese to Greek, Japanese to Polish, Thai to Lebanese. To a far greater degree than many other major cities, London's restaurants provide the opportunity to sample dishes from all around the world. The flowering of such a cosmopolitan array of eateries is evidence of a growing sophistication in British tastes – people are simply better travelled and better informed about food than ever before. At the same time this breadth of culinary influence has resulted in the birth of 'fusion' cooking, blending the flavours and ingredients of different traditions. At its worst, fusion cooking can be a nasty collision course, an exercise in meaningless sensation; at its best, it can be truly original. And here London has made its mark.

London's arrival on the world gastronomic stage is a fairly recent phenomenon and is inextricably linked to the property recession of the late 1980s and early 1990s when banks and other commercial institutions began to pull out of the high street and rents suffered a dramatic drop. The sudden availability and affordability of such prime locations coincided with the rise of a new type of entrepreneur who was increasingly attracted to the investment potential of the restaurant business. Restaurants, of course, are far from risk-free enterprises, and a huge proportion fail within months of opening. What they do offer, however, is the sense of participating in the cultural life of the city. The feeling of shared ownership can be a very powerful incentive for investors who would otherwise be conducting deals with faceless brokers on the other end of a fax, telephone or e-mail. Nowadays, as London has become a truly multicultural society, entrepreneurs from different cultures are also increasingly keen to promote their ideas about food to Londoners who are increasingly keen to sample them.

Although inherently chancy, investing in a restaurant is not quite a shot in the dark. One of the reasons why restaurant and café society is booming in London is that more people are choosing to socialize in this way. The restaurant is no longer the scene of intermittent celebration, but serves as a place where people can regularly enjoy a shared experience. At a time when more and more people live alone and often work in isolation in front of a screen, going out to eat or drink becomes an essential part of many social lives. It's a trend that professional forecasters, such as the Henley Centre, have projected will only continue.

My own career as a restaurant owner spans more or less the entire postwar period. I caught the bug at an early age and it has never left my bloodstream. My first restaurant was the Soup Kitchen which opened in 1953 – this was essentially a café serving a limited menu of soup, fresh bread, espresso, cheese and apple flan. I had conceived the idea when working in Paris as a *plongeur* at the famous restaurant La Méditerranée. Although I was utterly smitten by restaurant life, I was much less impressed by the casual brutality of restaurant chefs. The Soup Kitchen's simple fare was designed not only to appeal to young people who could not afford lavish three-course meals, but also as a way of avoiding having to employ and work with one of these kitchen tyrants.

The Soup Kitchen ventures (we eventually opened four) were followed by Orrery, at the 'wrong' end of the King's Road. This time there was a chef, an eccentric Pole who slept on the ice-cream fridge. We served omelettes and grilled Mediterranean-style food; the courtyard at the rear proved extremely popular for those unaccustomed to the pleasures of eating outdoors. Later, in 1971, I opened The Neal Street Restaurant, which is still going strong under the ownership of Antonio Carluccio, my brother-in-law. The Neal Street Restaurant began as a way of entertaining clients – my design business was then based in this Covent Garden street. But its success, at a time when Covent Garden was still a

The Michelin Building in Brompton Cross, which I renovated in collaboration with the publisher Paul Hamlyn, provided an early opportunity to combine eating with retailing. Bibendum, the restaurant above The Conran Shop, has won consistently high ratings.

littered and decrepit market area that had been given notice to move, also revealed the way in which restaurants, like shops, can be in the vanguard of regeneration, opening up new areas of the city.

Bibendum, which opened in 1987, represented a more ambitious venture, gastronomically speaking, and has since been consistently rated among the best restaurants in London. Located in the newly renovated Michelin Building, Bibendum formed part of a development that included The Conran Shop, a forecourt florist, an oyster bar and publisher's offices. The same idea of clustering eating and retail opportunities was behind my Butlers Wharf 'gastrodrome', with its four restaurants and specialist food shops, and my development of Bluebird in the King's Road, which combines on one site a restaurant, café, a food market, cook's shop and member's club. Food undoubtedly adds a 'feel good' factor to the experience of shopping – one has only to look at the increasing number of in-store coffee bars and restaurants for proof.

When I opened Bibendum a critic remarked that there could not possibly be room for another restaurant in London. The launch of Quaglino's – a huge space of 15,000 square feet off Jermyn Street – provoked even more disbelief. How could such a large restaurant expect ever to be successful? There could not possibly be that many people who wanted to go out to eat. The fact that Quaglino's opened in the depths of the recession only fuelled the scepticism – when money was so tight, why on earth would people want to go out and celebrate?

Quaglino's – big, buzzy and glamorous – proved just the tonic for the times. Modelled on the large Parisian brasseries, it was one of the first of a new wave of large London restaurants. I think that I would now be prepared to accept that large restaurants are nearing saturation point, certainly in the West End; and central London as a whole is probably oversupplied with restaurants of all sizes (although many could be replaced by restaurants that offer great food at affordable prices). The continuing success of Quaglino's, Mezzo and other large-scale restaurants such as Titanic or the Atlantic Bar and Grill provides the best possible evidence for the fact that Londoners now view going out to drink, eat and listen to music as a serious alternative to an evening at the cinema or theatre.

Impeccable service, simple hearty food and a regular seasoning of celebrities makes The Ivy near Cambridge Circus a perennial favourite.

If London restaurants today offer every conceivable type of cooking, they have also become much more sophisticated in design and ambience. Restaurant interiors were among the first to display the shift in taste away from fussy period decor, laden with chintz and swags, in favour of a more classic modern look. In the process there has been an increased cross-fertilization between home design and the design of restaurant, bar and hotel interiors. Domestic kitchens, for example, copy the professionalism of their restaurant counterparts, while restaurant kitchens have become more open and more integrated with the dining space.

The rise of the London restaurant has coincided with the fall of its more traditional venue, the pub. Once, every Londoner had his or her local, which, in the nature of things, was not necessarily the nearest public house to where they lived or worked, but a place where they felt at ease. Pub life was part of London mythology; so many East End boozers have been identified as the former local of the Kray twins, the notorious Sixties gangsters, that if they had drunk in all of them their criminal activities would have been severely curtailed. Nowadays, however, London is losing an average of two pubs a week. Such closures are the result of a change in drinking habits; competition from branded chains, such as the ubiquitous All Bar One or Pitcher and Piano; and the huge rise in property prices that means breweries can make a tidy profit selling off their licensed premises for conversion to residential use.

But there is another factor at play. The old 'spit and sawdust' pub, despite its nostalgic associations with Cockney knees-ups and singalongs, simply does not have the same appeal for a generation that prefers its beer bottled, ice-cold and European. Today's pub-goers do favour a rather more contemporary setting than a snug bar which looks like it last saw a paintbrush in 1952.

While there are pubs scattered around the city whose historic character is simply too strong to be overcome by a momentary eclipse – and there are signs that the fusty atmosphere of the traditional pub is becoming fashionable again – those that have survived generally offer something extra. The Eagle in Farringdon Road, near Clerkenwell, regularly tops the polls for the excellence of its rustic Italian cooking. My son Tom has had a similar success with The Cow, a pub in Westbourne Park Road that specializes in Irish food and drink. The King's Head in

The Travellers' Club in Pall Mall was founded in 1819 as a place where gentlemen who had been abroad could meet. The club house was designed to resemble an Italian Renaissance palace.

Islington has a theatre attached and until not too long ago was famous for quoting bar prices in old pre-decimalization money. The French House in Soho, formerly the York Minster but always known as 'The French', was the gathering place of the Free French during the Second World War and now has an excellent dining room above, serving modern British cooking.

One London institution that has enjoyed a surprising revival of fortunes, is the members-only club. London still has its gentleman's clubs, some of which remain bastions of class prejudice and male chauvinism, and many of which are spectacular architecturally. I particularly enjoy the atmosphere of the Travellers' Club in Pall Mall, designed by Charles Barry in the form of an Italian Renaissance palace. Architecture alone, however, is not enough to prevent membership from dwindling. The fate of the old Naval and Military Club on Piccadilly – always known as the In and Out Club from the signs painted on the entrance and exit gates – is symptomatic: the club has been forced to relocate from the premises it has occupied for more than 130 years and the building has recently been sold for conversion into private accommodation.

In the past 15 years a new type of club has appeared in London. Offering the same comfort of 'belonging' but essentially much more democratic in spirit, these clubs are defiantly metropolitan in atmosphere, whereas the old clubs preserved the feeling – and the furnishings – of the country house. The Groucho Club, where media people network, set the trend when it opened in Soho in 1985 – the name refers to Groucho Marx's quip that he would never join a club that would have him as a member. Many others, including Black's, Soho House and Two Brydges Place, have followed suit.

It's not quite 'Time, please!' for the traditional London pub but new bar chains are encroaching on the same territory.

Hotels, in many ways, serve as the public face of a city, both providing a home from home for visitors and projecting an image of the host country that they expect to see. In the past many London hotels were either decorated to look like a subspecies of country house – all pot pourri, chintz and reproduction furniture – or were of the faceless 'international' variety, the type that seems to state: 'If it's Tuesday, it must be …'. But times have changed. The most recent development on the eating-and-drinking scene is the arrival of the so-called 'boutique' hotel, which offers a choice of restaurants, bars and members-only clubs under one roof. These new destinations, aimed at Londoners and weekenders as much as longer-stay visitors to the capital, combine innovative contemporary design with the latest technological features and services.

Ian Schrager, the New York entrepreneur responsible for the Royalton, among many others, has recently launched St Martins Lane and the Sanderson in London. Schrager is generally credited with both the concept and the term 'boutique hotel'. But London was no stranger to the idea. Blakes, opened by Anoushka Hempel in the 1970s, was among the first to employ an almost theatrical style of decoration and won a devoted celebrity following. Her more recent venture, The Hempel, which opened in 1995, is an equally dramatic temple to Zen, with its austere atrium, meticulously arranged orchids and fibreoptic-lit taps.

Two things mark out the current new wave of hotels as different: their scale and their determination to serve as 'pleasure palaces' (another Schrager term) for Londoners and hotel guests alike. The Metropolitan on Park Lane, owned by Christina Ong, is the location of Nobu, one of London's most successful fusion restaurants, and of the celebrity-filled Met Bar (members only at night). One Aldwych offers contemporary luxury in an Edwardian building that was once the headquarters of the *Morning Post*. Among countless amenities, it has its own private screening room. St Martins Lane, designed by Philippe Starck, features another fusion restaurant, Asia de Cuba. Rooms have 'interactive' lighting that enables guests to adjust the colour according to their mood.

People have shown that they enjoy going out to modern restaurants, so why not modern hotels? Our revival of the Great Eastern Hotel, near Liverpool Street – astonishingly the only hotel in the City until now – has been designed to marry the grandeur of its Victorian architecture with a simpler, more contemporary quality. At the same time, the intention has not merely been to woo overseas or weekend visitors but to provide a focus for the daily activity of a bustling part of London. Traditionally hotel restaurants tended to be buried in the heart of the building, which sent out a message of exclusivity. At the Great Eastern the various restaurants and bars – which range from the upmarket Aurora to the Terminus brasserie, The Fishmarket or The George pub to the Japanese food bar Miyabi – have their own independent entrances that serve to break through to and connect with the surrounding streets.

Food and drink in London used to mean warm beer, grey meat, overboiled vegetables, chips with everything and, what is more, odd opening hours. Today it is just as likely to be Thai takeaway, sushi delivered on a conveyor belt, a frothing caffè latte, or a Vodka Stinger sipped from a perch at one of the capital's latest late-night bars. The warm beer and chips have not disappeared, of course, but at least Londoners now have a choice – and a huge one at that.

A vast rotunda in the heart of the Great Eastern Hotel – affectionately known as 'baby Guggenheim' – brings dramatic views and a sense of theatre to the reception area.

OVERLEAF: Sunday morning dim sum in the New World Chinese restaurant, Soho.

For all the technological wizardry they offer, internet cafes can be dreary affairs, with row upon row of terminals and not much else in the way of visual excitement. Nutopia in Covent Garden (LEFT) is a striking exception. Designer Grant Mitchell has endeavoured to create an environment that is as up-to-the-minute as the brave new world of cyberspace, through the use of projected images, low lighting and a changing programme of art installations – including the light sculpture made of three skipping ropes by Paul Friedlander shown here. The Vibe Bar in Brick Lane is one of a number of new places to drink and be seen that have sprung up as the fashion focus falls on east London (ABOVE).

For 50 years, the Colony Room in Soho has been a home from home for generations of British artists, including Lucian Freud, Francis Bacon, Frank Auerbach and Patrick Caulfield, together with more recent devotees Damien Hirst and Sarah Lucas (ABOVE). Rather more respectable, but the scene of equally memorable bohemian excesses is the Chelsea Arts Club, whose founder members included Whistler and Walter Sickert (RIGHT).

Plenty of Londoners still prefer their fish well fried and battered, and accompanied, in the time-honoured fashion, with a generous helping of chips (LEFT) but an increasing number are also prepared to try it raw, with a little wasabi. Yo! Sushi in Poland Street offers sushi and sashimi in a Japanese-style canteen.

Huge on atmosphere, Bar Italia in Soho evokes those heady days in the 1950s when a cappuccino was the last word in sophistication (LEFT). The New Piccadilly Café has a similar retro charm (RIGHT, TOP AND BOTTOM). The Bonnington Square Café in Vauxhall began life as a corner shop and then became a communal café, the social hub of an eclectic community of local residents who first moved in to squat in the square's empty houses 20 years ago (BELOW).

There are said to be more Indian restaurants in London than the whole of Bombay and Delhi combined, a statistic that is no doubt a source of some pride for the staff at the Star of India, Old Brompton Road (ABOVE). Claridges in Brook Street retains its reputation as a hotel restaurant of some cachet (ABOVE LEFT).

Relative newcomers on the restaurant scene reflect London's status on the international gastronomic map. The Oxo Tower restaurant, on the eighth floor of this South Bank landmark, provides diners with a stunning panorama of the city (LEFT). The innovative menu at Moro in Exmouth Market is influenced by the cooking of Spain and North Africa (BELOW LEFT). Kensington Place in west London was one of the first modern British brasseries (BELOW).

OVERLEAF: The incomparable J Sheekeys in St Martins Court is just the place to go if the month has an 'R' in it.

Over 400 staff cater for the needs of guests staying at the Great Eastern, our hotel near Liverpool Street Station in the City. The main reception area (CENTRE) is an oasis of calm that belies the constant bustle behind the scenes – from morning bedmaking and food deliveries to the spectacular choreography as the hotel's restaurant kitchens swing into action.

LEFT: The Rookery, a hotel tucked away near Smithfield Market on the fringes of the City, consists of a group of restored houses, furnished with original furniture and beds, such as this elaborately carved eighteenth-century four-poster. 'Rookery' was the Victorian term for the dense alleyways and courts where both crime and poverty were rife.

RIGHT: At St Martins Lane, 'interactive' lighting allows guests to change the colour of their room to suit their mood or the time of day. The first Schrager hotel in London, St Martins Lane, was designed by Philippe Starck.

PREVIOUS PAGES: Compared to the stately grandeur of the Ritz (RIGHT) the reception area at St Martins Lane is proof of a seismic shift in hotel design in the capital (LEFT).

Green London

One night when returning to London after a trip abroad I noticed a sea of black amid the city's many points of light as the aeroplane began its descent ready for landing at Heathrow. It took me a while to work out that this vast dark expanse was actually Richmond Park. The realization brought home to me just how much green space London has right on its doorstep.

Londoners themselves may often find themselves focusing on the negative features of the city's environment – the litter, the graffiti, the car-choked streets – but visitors are often surprised by how much greenery there is right in the heart of the capital: not only parks, but shady squares and shrubberies; roads lined with London's characteristic tree, the plane; roof terraces crammed with pots of plants; and back gardens abundant with flowers and vegetables.

One explanation must be that deep-rooted British affection for the countryside, the persistent desire to connect with nature – even if the only space available is a windowbox. The crowds that throng the annual horticultural highlights of the Chelsea and Hampton Court flower shows, the bargain-hunters who pack the plant and flower market at Columbia Road every Sunday, and the brisk trade at countless nurseries and garden centres tucked away in backstreet yards prove that many Londoners take their gardening very seriously indeed. The last day of the Chelsea Flower Show provides much incidental amusement when the surrounding streets are suddenly transformed into what looks like a Shakespearean Birnam Wood or a huge garden on the move, but what is, in reality, people staggering away laden down with their leafy purchases.

The great plant collections at the Royal Botanic Gardens at Kew and the Chelsea Physic Garden, one of my personal favourites, provide much inspiration for the city gardener. Kew was founded in the early eighteenth century and included specimens collected by Captain Cook; there are now 33,000 different species in the gardens and in planthouses. The Palm House alone, designed by Decimus Burton in the 1840s, houses 3,000 species. Kew occupies some 300 acres; rather more intimate – and possibly more inspiring for that reason – is the physic garden at Chelsea, the oldest in the country after the botanic garden in Oxford. Chelsea was established in 1676 and is still, like Kew, a centre of research. Comprising only four acres planted with rare species, including what is thought to be the oldest olive tree in the country, the garden encloses you almost like a secret world.

LEFT: Green Park was first enclosed by Henry VIII. It is believed that the reason no flowers grow here is because it is the site of a former leper burial ground. It now provides a pleasant escape from the grime of the main Piccadilly thoroughfare.

ABOVE: The Chelsea Physic Garden is one of my favourite green spaces.

Other hidden treasures include garden squares. When large areas of west London were developed in the seventeenth and eighteenth centuries by speculative builders, aristocratic landowners often insisted on the provision of communal space for the surrounding residents. These garden squares, which contribute such a civilizing element to central London, are still maintained by private associations but now open their gates at least once a year to the general public.

During the Second World War, when Britain was exhorted to 'dig for victory', many of London's ornamental gardens, both private and public, were transformed into vegetable plots and hen runs. No site was too grand to serve this essential utilitarian purpose: cabbages and potatoes were even planted around the Queen Victoria Memorial in front of Buckingham Palace. London gardens today are more likely to serve as outdoor living areas than provide supplements for the larder, but the productive patch of the allotment is, if anything, more sought-after than ever before. Many councils have succumbed to commercial pressures and sold off land formerly devoted to allotments, but the huge waiting lists for plots in some areas indicate that a new generation of young gardeners are keen to experience the satisfaction of growing their own, and keen to taste the difference between real fresh vegetables and the hydroponically grown Dutch varieties available in the supermarket.

From the productive allotment to container-grown displays on doorsteps, windowsills and roofs, the private garden provides plenty of opportunity for creative and sometimes eccentric expression. But equally important are the public breathing spaces, London's green 'lungs'. In medieval times the city was surrounded by a great forest, a wilderness that harboured wild boar, wild bulls and wolves; a few ancient oaks dating from this period can still be seen in some of London's parks. The fact that these parks – and their oaks – have managed to survive centuries of urban development has a great deal to do with Henry VIII's passion for hunting.

St James's Park, the oldest of London's royal parks, was originally marshland until Henry VIII had it drained and enclosed. He subsequently commandeered the burial ground of a leper's hospital (now Green Park)

Boating on the lake in St James's Park, the oldest of London's royal parks. In the eighteenth century, cows were kept tethered in the park and visitors could buy mugs of fresh warm milk at a penny a time.

and helped himself to vast tracts of land owned by the Church after the Dissolution (Hyde Park and Regent's Park). Henry's intention was to create an almost continuous stretch of royal playground for hunting, 'maying', mock battles and tournaments. Although these pleasures were then exclusive to the Court, it is largely thanks to these acquisitions that a green belt of land runs right the way through central London for the enjoyment of the public today.

Victoria Park in Hackney, which opened in 1845, was the first public park in London.

Greenwich Park in southeast London was another favourite area of recreation for members of the Tudor Court, while the 2,500 acres of Richmond Park in southwest London was originally enclosed by Charles I for his own private use. Richmond, which is actually the largest city park in Europe, was given to the Corporation of London after the Civil War in recognition of the City's support for the Commonwealth. When Charles II was restored to the throne the City rather promptly gave it back again in a gesture of barefaced political expediency.

Although Richmond remained out of bounds right up until the reign of George II, many of the other royal parks had begun to admit the public much earlier. James I opened Hyde Park to the public, and by the eighteenth century it had become an extremely fashionable place in which to drive, ride or promenade. Rotten Row (thought to be a corruption of *route de roi*), a bridlepath connecting Kensington Palace with St James's, became the first lit road in England when William III had lamps hung from the trees to deter the highwaymen who preyed on rich courtiers. The Serpentine was created in 1730 under the instructions of Queen Caroline, who had the River Westbourne dammed to create an artificial lake; it was later the setting of a miniature re-enactment of the Battle of Trafalgar.

At the first hint of spring office workers make for London's parks in their lunchbreaks to eat their sandwiches, sunbathe, or wander around admiring the flowers (or each other's bodies); although the planting is often so predictable that I do wonder if there is a great municipal store of marigolds somewhere in the city! More riotous and spectacular amusements used to be on offer in the royal parks, among them fairs, ballooning and fireworks. Duels were fought in Green Park, and St James's became a notorious haunt of prostitutes and their customers. Until the end of the eighteenth century Tyburn Gallows, to the northeast of Hyde Park (now the site of Marble Arch), attracted huge crowds to that most unpleasant of London's spectator sports, the public hanging.

In addition to the royal parks, pleasure gardens began to appear in the seventeenth century, the most popular being Vauxhall in Lambeth and the more exclusive Ranelagh in Chelsea, where fashionable society could stroll through the lamplit grounds, take part in masquerades, have supper at pavilions or listen to music. The pleasure gardens charged for admission, a tactic designed to keep out undesirable elements as much as raise money. Nevertheless, pleasure gardens eventually provided an ideal environment for what could best be described as general debauchery.

The Victorians took rather a different view of open space, with the ruling classes believing the public park provided the opportunity to wean the lower classes off unhealthy pleasures – drinking gin and watching dogfights, for example – and introduce them to the benefits of sport and fresh air. The first public, as opposed to royal, park was Victoria Park in east London, opened in 1845; the second was Battersea, in 1853. Gradually over the centuries, but increasingly since the coming of industrialization and the railways, many of London's unofficial open spaces – patches of land where livestock once grazed – had disappeared under development. All that remained to indicate that Stepney Green or Moorfields, for example, were once green fields, were their names. The efforts of the reforming Victorians came just in time to preserve at least some green space for the millions who lived outside the city centre.

What such reformers envisaged was moral improvement, but parks also offered the opportunity for political dissent and public demonstration. Soon after it opened, Victoria Park was the scene of a Chartists' demonstration in 1848; later there were rousing political rallies addressed by George Bernard Shaw and William Morris. Some 150,000 gathered in Hyde Park to protest against the Sunday Trading Bill in 1855 – a demonstration, incidentally, witnessed by Karl Marx – which prompted the authorities to set aside the northeast corner of the park as Speakers' Corner. Today this may attract the more evangelical and eccentric soapbox preachers, but Hyde Park also remains the main point of departure for those political marches that traditionally culminate in mass rallies in Trafalgar Square.

It was perhaps a similar sort of mass instinct that gripped the public in the wake of the death of Diana, Princess of Wales, and caused millions of flowers and tributes to be laid outside Crowther Gates, south of Kensington Palace. After seemingly endless deliberations about the precise nature of a more permanent London memorial, a new children's playground has now been created in Kensington Gardens on the site of an old play area that was originally funded by a donation from J. M. Barrie, author of *Peter Pan*. As well as areas where children can explore music and movement, there is a 'Tree-House Encampment' and a seven-tonne pirate ship in acknowledgement of the playground's early association with the playwright.

The Green Bridge, planted with trees, connects the north and south sides of Mile End Park, which was relandscaped and improved in a Lottery-funded scheme designed by architect Piers Gough and landscape architect Ros Brewer.

There is no doubt that a significant number of inner London's public parks have suffered somewhat over the past few decades. Their relative decline began during the Second World War when many of the city's parks and gardens were stripped of their iron railings, so that they could then be shipped off and melted down for use in the war industries. These iron railings have since proved prohibitively expensive to replace. Then, in the 1980s when local councils were encouraged to contract out essential services such as refuse collection and park maintainance, many park-keepers lost their jobs. One might compare a park without a warden to a bus without a conductor; as a result there has been a similar rise in vandalism and crime in both parks and on buses, an effect directly attributable to the lack of these essential human controls. And this again connects to the problems suffered by tower blocks with their lack of security. It remains a fact that human beings cannot successfully be replaced by security cameras.

Recently a number of London's parks have become Lottery beneficiaries under the auspices of the English Heritage Lottery Fund. Imaginative landscape and playground designs have been produced to revitalize what had become rather unkempt, litter-strewn and threatening urban spaces. Projects such as the Millennium Park in Mile End, which creates a green corridor from Victoria Park to the river, demonstrate a new ecological awareness: at Mile End a road bridge has been planted with huge container-grown trees. Other such schemes include those sponsored by Learning Through Landscapes, an organisation which has been instrumental in the greening of many London school playgrounds; and the charity Trees for London, that has been responsible for a new urban oak woodland at Merton that is well on target to fulfil its immediate aim of planting 20,000 trees in the city by 2001.

Perhaps the most visible urban regeneration of all has been the development of the Greenwich Peninsula, formerly one of the largest and most derelict industrial sites in the city. Once home to a gasworks and other chemical industries, the peninsula was heavily polluted with the dangerous residues and by-products of these processes, which, in the days before environmental controls, had simply been dumped *in situ*. When Greenwich was chosen in 1996 as the location for the millennial celebrations, the clean-up was already under way but it proved a race against the clock to transform a poisonous wasteground into a festival site. When I visited the Dome, which occupies the northern end of the peninsula, I was particularly impressed by the treatment of the outdoor areas. A derelict jetty a few metres from the riverbank has been planted with native wild species to form a habitat for waterfowl; the river edge has been 'greened' with shelving terraces to provide a place for fish to 'rest' and a lagoon of reeds has been planted to create natural filtration for recycling grey water.

Green space in London serves and has served many purposes, from royal playgrounds to places where the fashionable can promenade, from places of spontaneous assembly to places of refuge (200,000 sheltered in Highbury Fields during the Great Fire of London). Children who have never seen a sheep or a cow can visit one of London's city farms; would-be botanists can hunt down rare species in the famous plant collections of Kew and Chelsea. For those of a Gothic turn of mind, some of London's oldest cemeteries provide food for thought: Highgate Cemetery, where Bram Stoker was inspired to write *Dracula*, features spectacularly overgrown mausoleums and family tombs, although its most famous resident is undoubtedly Karl Marx.

For most of us, however, green London simply provides an essential safety valve for the tensions that naturally arise in the frantic daily life of a huge city, and is all the more valuable for being unstructured and spontaneous. Traditional London is 'red' – but its skies and buildings are undoubtedly often grey. Yet whether it be the sudden uplifting sight of a flowering cherry or magnolia as you hurry by on the pavement, a breathless game of many-a-side football in the local park, with plane trees bursting into leaf, or an hour spent playfully kicking up leaves on Hampstead Heath, some of London's happiest moments are green.

Improvised goal on the end of a terrace in Kilburn.

OVERLEAF: Winter in St James's Park, which provides an urban sanctuary for migrating geese and waterfowl. There have been pelicans in the park ever since a pair was presented to Charles II.

PREVIOUS PAGES: A Georgian doorway in Islington dappled with light (LEFT); container gardening at the Golden Lane Estate in the City (RIGHT).

Strong on discipline and immaculately tasteful, the Japanese-inspired garden of this house designed by
Seth Stein makes use of grasses to soften the lines of paving (ABOVE LEFT). Cheerful clutter and chaos,
along with a not-altogether-successful recycling of found objects, reveals a positively laid-back attitude
to nature in this east London garden (ABOVE). The plane tree, which provides shade for so many
London gardens and streets was introduced to England from Portugal in the late seventeenth century.
Its prevalence in London owes much to the fact that it can tolerate high levels of pollution.

In the heart of the city, greenery sprouts from surprising places. Roofs make difficult and exposed environments for gardening but the bonus for all the hard work and steep horticultural learning curves is great views: green fingers have been busy in these high-rise gardens in Battersea (LEFT) and Notting Hill Gate (ABOVE).

Every Sunday morning, Columbia Road in Hackney is the scene for some serious
shopping in the plant and flower market (ABOVE). Bargain-hunters also turn out
in droves to pick over the exhibits on the last day of the Chelsea Flower Show
(BELOW RIGHT). Chelsea's showstoppers are its individually created gardens.
Bucking the trend for garden glamour and precision finish, the Chelsea garden
made by inmates of Leyhill open prison presented an unusual gardening
viewpoint – and picked up a coveted medal at the 2000 show (ABOVE RIGHT).
The open doorway of the shed represents 'freedom'; the robust wild flowers and
weeds symbolize society's outcasts.

No greater antidote to urban stress exists than the allotment, the scene of much gentle rumination and strenuous double-digging. Allotments on the fringes of the city at Dulwich (ABOVE AND RIGHT) and Fulham Palace (TOP) reveal certain common characteristics: a thrifty way with old window frames and recycled building materials, quiet companionship and spectacular views.

LEFT: A desolate East End site, under a looming gasometer, has been transformed by artist-gardener Gavin Jones into a community garden. He decided to plough the land with Shire horses rather than a tractor to arouse local interest in the project; the strip has now been planted with poppies, corn marigolds and blue linseed.

ABOVE: The Sky Pavilion, designed by artist Henna Nadeem and David Adjaye, for the Limehouse Fields Estate, poetically re-creates the dappled effect of light shining through a canopy of leaves.

The Royal Botanic Gardens at Kew is a world-leading centre of botanical research, which attracts a million-odd annual visitors to view the variety and beauty of its displays. The Palm House, designed by Decimus Burton in the 1840s, is both an architectural and botanical draw (ABOVE AND RIGHT). The Princess of Wales Conservatory, opened in 1987, is a more recent addition; here a Kew gardener tends some of its giant water lilies (FAR RIGHT).

A lazy summer's afternoon at Highgate Ponds on Hampstead Heath.

In keeping with the Zen minimalism of her latest hotel, the Hempel, Anoushka Hempel has designed the square which forms the hotel's garden as an essay in geometry (LEFT). Arabella Lennox-Boyd's design for the rooftop garden at Coq d'Argent, my restaurant in the City, makes dramatic use of formal arrangement and outdoor lighting (ABOVE).

OVERLEAF: Bill Woodrow's towering bronze sculpture of a tree, *Regardless of History*, takes up temporary residence on Trafalgar Square's 'empty' plinth (LEFT) beautifully mirrored by an angel in Kensal Rise Cemetery (RIGHT).

Every Christmas a huge Christmas tree is erected in Trafalgar Square, the gift of the people of Norway in gratitude for Britain's assistance during the Second World War (LEFT). Members of the Polar Bear Club line up for their annual Christmas Day swim in the Serpentine, Hyde Park (ABOVE). The Serpentine is a lake created for Queen Caroline in the early eighteenth century by damming the Westbourne, one of London's lost rivers.

OVERLEAF: A winter's outing to Greenwich Park, southeast London.

Time Out

I have borrowed the title of this chapter from London's most popular weekly listings guide – not as an act of barefaced cheek, but in simple acknowledgement of the fact that there is no better way to review the vast range of amusements that the city has to offer. The briefest glance at the contents page of *Time Out* confirms that London provides just about every conceivable form of entertainment: from greyhound racing to arthouse cinema, from kite-flying to clubbing, from gazing at Old Masters to gazing at pickled sheep in tanks. Samuel Johnson observed that '… when a man is tired of London, he is tired of life', a remark that has become the most frequently quoted comments on the city. On the other hand, anyone who has attempted to sample even a fraction of what is on in the city every week would be bound to need an early night now and again.

Diversity is inevitable when there are so many different cultural tastes to satisfy and a ready market of pleasure-seekers. If basic distinctions can be drawn between the mainstream and the elite, between highbrow and lowbrow attractions, those for the young and those for the not-so-young, there is an even more fundamental divide between the way that Londoners and tourists choose to entertain themselves. In common with the inhabitants of most major cities, people who live in London tend to be fairly indifferent to the sights that draw visitors from further afield. I suspect that surprisingly few Londoners have been to the Tower of London, queued up for a peek inside Buckingham Palace or gone out of their way to see the Changing of the Guard. The true Londoner is far more likely to line the routes of the capital to watch the Marathon or the Notting Hill Carnival than a state occasion such as Trooping the Colour.

Londoners, however, may be missing out without realizing it. Not long ago I was invited by the Keeper of the Royal Fabric to look round the Tower, which turned out to be a marvellous behind-the-scenes tour of this medieval fortress and village, commissioned soon after the Battle of Hastings by William the Conqueror as a way of impressing upon his newly

ABOVE: Competitors in the London Marathon pour across Tower Bridge.

LEFT: A fairground at dusk in Hyde Park.

conquered subjects the might of Norman rule. When I eventually returned to work (which is only a ten-minute walk away) a quick straw poll revealed that hardly anyone in the office had visited the Tower since childhood, despite the fact that it really is one of the most extraordinary places in London.

London's reliance on the tourist industry is a fairly recent phenomenon, but, as Samuel Johnson's remark reveals, the city has been a pleasure ground for many, many centuries. If some of the diversions have disappeared without trace – bear-baiting and cock-fighting were once particularly popular blood-sports in the capital – others have demonstrated considerable staying power. Notable among these is theatre-going, an activity traditionally associated with the capital and one of the longest survivors in the roll call of its many entertainments.

The first commercial concerts were not performed in London until the middle of the seventeenth century; the first museums began to appear a century later, only when it became fashionable to collect antiques. But London's first purpose-built playhouse, The Theatre in Shoreditch, was founded by James Burbage in 1576. When the lease on the original site ran out after Burbage's death some 20 years later, his sons simply dismantled the theatre and had the timbers rowed across the river where

The reconstructed Globe Theatre, on its original site in Southwark.

they were promptly used to construct the Globe. In 1602, the year Shakespeare completed *All's Well That Ends Well*, it is estimated that London's theatres had an average daily attendance of 5,000.

This first flowering of London theatre, which lasted about 70 years, saw playhouses become fashionable places of assembly, where people gathered to see and be seen. Courtiers and gentry rubbed shoulders with students and apprentices, prostitutes and cut-purses, to enjoy the works of dramatists such as Shakespeare, Ben Jonson and Christopher Marlowe. The recent reconstruction of the Globe – Shakespeare's 'wooden O' – on its original site at Southwark, a labour of love nurtured by the late American actor Sam Wanamaker, has revived the physical framework of the Elizabethan theatre; its inclusive spirit proves rather more difficult to recapture.

Despite royal patronage, the popularity of Elizabethan and Jacobean theatre gave the high-minded cause for concern. The first theatres were all located outside the bounds of the city, as were most of London's brothels, which gave rise to many obvious associations.

Audiences could be boisterous and bawdy, sometimes riotous. After the Civil War, during the Commonwealth, theatre-going was banned by the Puritans; when theatres reopened after the Restoration, new controls were in place. At the end of the seventeenth century there were only two theatres that were permitted to produce full-length dramas: the Theatre Royal, Drury Lane and the Theatre Royal, Covent Garden, which later became the Royal Opera House.

By this time the potential of the theatre to act as a focus for political unrest was causing more concern than its previous reputation as the home of immorality. The Licensing Act of 1737 gave the Lord Chamberlain draconian powers of censorship, powers that were revoked only in 1968. Controls, however, have never proved entirely effective when it comes to regulating the way people want to enjoy themselves. Some theatres found a way round the restrictions by putting on mixed bills, spectacles that included parts of plays, singing and novelty acts, a popular form of entertainment that reached its peak in the variety programmes of the nineteenth-century music hall.

The foundations of West End theatreland – which continues to draw both tourists and Londoners, although not necessarily to the same shows – were laid in the second half of the nineteenth century. Seven new theatres were built around the Strand in the 1860s and double that number between the 1880s and 1890s. The great actor-managers such as Henry Irving and Beerbohm Tree wooed middle-class audiences with Shakespearean revivals, while the works of provocative new playwrights such as Shaw and Ibsen were also staged. Lavishly appointed with saloon bars and lounges and richly decorated in red velvet and gilt, these turn-of-the-century playhouses were sumptuous palaces of entertainment for well to do, educated audiences. Theatre-going gained a new respectability, despite the fact that they still looked a bit like rather smart bordellos.

The history of the Royal Court theatre in Sloane Square, built in 1888, provides an illustration of the changing fortunes of London's playhouses in the twentieth century. In the three years between 1904 and 1907 32 plays by 17 different playwrights were produced at the Royal Court; many of Shaw's plays, including *Candida* and *Major Barbara* premiered here. But just a few decades later the theatre was at a low ebb; it closed in 1932, became a cinema in 1934 and was bombed in 1940. After rebuilding in the early 1950s the new Royal Court became the home of the English Stage Company, responsible for many ground-breaking productions, including *Look Back in Anger*, in 1956. By the 1990s, however, despite its international reputation as a forcing ground for new writing talent, the theatre itself was in

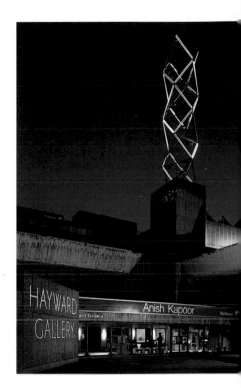

Ron Haselden's kinetic light sculpture at the Hayward Gallery on the South Bank reacts to wind speed. Architect Rick Mather has recently been commissioned to 'masterplan' the entire South Bank complex.

exceptionally poor repair, condemned as dangerously unsafe. Now, rescued by a Lottery grant (supplemented by private donations) the theatre has recently reopened after four years of extensive renovation.

What is particularly interesting about the Royal Court, however, is the nature of its revival and the way this highlights certain key issues regarding the treatment of historic buildings. Some of London's theatres have been restored to within an inch of their lives, their jewelbox but curiously sterile interiors providing another attraction on the heritage trail. Others, notably Sadler's Wells, have been reincarnated in brand-new buildings that offer the modern accommodation required by performing companies and audiences alike. The renovation of the Royal Court, by architects Haworth Tomkins, demonstrates an intriguing alternative. Their solution, which seems to combine the best of both worlds, has been to treat the original building almost like an archaeological site, peeling back superficial layers of twentieth-century decoration to reveal the robustness of the underlying Victorian construction. At the same time, modern facilities have been integrated so sensitively that it is difficult to see the join. Exposed iron beams, builders' marks and the odd trace of bomb damage provide a uniquely textural background that is steeped in the theatre's illustrious history but does not in any way fall into the 'heritage' trap. A new café and restaurant are sited in the extended basement; the theatre has new seating and appropriately atmospheric lighting. The result has been to keep what matters – an almost indefinable sense of community – while providing a properly functioning context for performance.

At the Royal Court the message is that the quality of the productions is what counts. Elsewhere in theatreland things are not so rosy. Seven out of nine West End shows fail; most of London's theatres are now in the hands of either the Ambassadors Theatre Group (which owns 11) or Andrew Lloyd Webber's Really Useful Group (which owns 13). The huge costs of staging productions, the escalation in property values and dwindling and ageing audiences are creating a difficult climate for high-quality, provocative new works. The success of productions at small theatres such as Islington's Almeida, or the Donmar Warehouse where Nicole Kidman recently performed in David Hare's *The Blue Room* to great acclaim, proves that audiences are still hungry for serious drama and are not irretrievably dumbed down.

The recent crisis in theatre-going may seem like a fringe issue when you consider all the other attractions London has to offer. But I believe it is worthy of concern because, in many ways, providing these types of shared experience is precisely what cities are for. First television, then later video and then films downloaded from the internet were all supposed

ABOVE: Nicole Kidman and Iain Glen in *The Blue Room*, written by David Hare and directed by Sam Mendes at the Donmar Warehouse.

FAR RIGHT: The idiosyncratic Sir John Soane's Museum in Lincoln's Inn Fields is a walk-in cabinet of curiosities.

to spell the end of cinema-going. Yet cinema attendance in London remains good and there has even been an upturn in the fortunes of the repertory or arthouse cinema, offering a serious alternative to nationally distributed blockbusters. The reasons seem pretty obvious: films are funnier, sadder, more powerful and altogether more cinematic (despite the popcorn) when you are watching them in the dark with scores of other people than when you view them on a small screen in the corner of your living room.

Some of London's picture houses qualify as heritage buildings, although few of these still function as cinemas. Early picture palaces, built in the great wave of cinema-building in the 1920s and 1930s, were precisely that: glorious architectural fantasies that ushered audiences, who had never set foot outside London, into an exotic world. The 'Alhambras' that managed to survive with their Art Deco façades intact were those that found a new use as bingo halls; some are now listed. Other, smaller cinemas have managed to retain a loyal local audience: the Phoenix in East Finchley, with its prewar atmosphere, was recently used as a location in Neil Jordan's adaptation of Graham Greene's *The End of the Affair*. New London cinemas, such as the Lux in Hoxton, along with private screening rooms and cinema clubs, strive to offer a greater sense of comfort and a stronger identity than the bland shoebox of the multiplex. From *Notting Hill* to *Lock, Stock and Four Smoking Barrels*, the fact that London itself has been portrayed in many recent film successes has only intensified the interest.

The old picture palaces inspired affection; palaces of high culture, on the other hand, are often the focus of ferocious debate. Even before the Prince of Wales branded the proposed extension to the National Gallery as a 'monstrous carbuncle on the face of a much-loved friend', museums, public galleries and arts complexes — from the Royal National Theatre to the new British Library — have aroused great controversy. The vituperation that greeted Daniel Liebeskind's *Spiral*, the proposed new wing of the V&A, for example, conceals a deeper unease arising from a lack of consensus about what the contemporary role of these cultural institutions should be.

Many of London's great museums originated as collections of private individuals – cabinets of curiosities that outgrew their cabinets. The British Museum, which first opened to the public in 1759, comprised three principal collections that had been donated or sold to the nation: art, antiquities and natural history collections amassed by Sir Hans Sloan; manuscripts from the library of Robert Harley, 1st Earl of Oxford; and a library and antiquities collected by the Cotton family. The National Gallery, founded in 1824, brought together 38 paintings collected by John Julius Angerstein, a merchant, and 16 pictures donated

to the nation by the connoisseur Sir George Beaumont. Something of the intimate scale and flavour of these early museums can still be experienced in one of my favourite places in London, the delightfully eccentric Sir John Soane's Museum in Lincoln's Inn Fields. This treasure trove houses the architect's personal collection of casts, marbles, classical fragments and works of art, along with many other curios, including an Egyptian sarcophagus, Sir Christopher Wren's watch and Napoleon's pistol. The delight that permeates the museum is not merely a result of its unique architectural character, it also owes much to the fact that the passion with which the collection was first assembled is still palpable.

The Soane Museum is unusual in its idiosyncrasy. Other London collections have simply grown and grown, the curatorial function long since overwhelming individual flavour. Most can now display only a fraction of what they have acquired in the nation's interest. The V&A, founded with the proceeds of the Great Exhibition of 1851, was intended to have an educational purpose, demonstrating and promoting 'the influence of Science and Art upon Productive Industry', but successive acquisitions strayed some considerable way from this central intention until it became what one former director, Sir Roy Strong, termed 'an extremely capacious handbag'. I was a trustee of the museum for 13 years and can confirm there is very little evidence of rational direction when one looks at the sheer quantity and oddity of what has been acquired over the 150 years of the museum's history, much of which has very little to do with the founding purpose.

The Buckminster Fuller exhibition at the Design Museum. Three major exhibitions are held at the museum each year, alongside a permanent collection and a gallery of new designs and innovations.

When I established the Conran Foundation, a charitable foundation with the aim of promoting design education and enlightenment in 1981, an emerging crisis in arts funding was fuelling the debate between those who wanted museums to be academic storehouses, preserving the nation's treasures (and very often, as in the case of the 'British' Museum and the Elgin Marbles, other nations' treasures), and those who sought more public accessibility. In 1982 we put the aims of the Foundation into practice with the launch of the Boilerhouse project, 5,000 square feet of exhibition space located in the old boilerhouse yard of the V&A. The Boilerhouse had five extremely successful years, mounting a succession of exhibitions dedicated to demonstrating the importance of design in both manufacturing and everyday life. Then, in 1989, we opened the Design Museum at Butlers Wharf in a modern conversion of a 1950s warehouse – a design, incidentally, that the Prince of Wales liked no better than any of the other contemporary buildings that had previously incurred his invective.

The Design Museum, the only permanent collection and exhibition of modern design in Britain, has more than fulfilled its educational role. And we have tried to incorporate the flavour of an individual collection by asking a different personality to make their own selection of work every year. But the museum can only survive by attracting corporate sponsorship. Many view the intrusion of commerce into the rarefied world of the museum with pure horror, just as they deplore the museum shop and museum café whose takings are increasingly necessary as a supplement to exhibition ticket sales. I believe, however, that such marriages can be managed successfully, particularly if there is a sympathetic match of sponsor and exhibition. Recent trends in exhibition design, in which the new buzz words are 'interactivity' and 'narrative', indicate that there is also a concern to make museums more accessible and involving for the public and especially schoolchildren. Too much button-pressing can be simply vapid, but imaginative ventures such as the hugely popular Science Nights at the Science Museum, when children treasure-hunt and sleep-over among the rockets and steam engines, stimulate a whole new way of experiencing museum collections.

The greatest change in London's cultural life, however, and the one that will have the most lasting impact on the fabric of the city, is the arrival of the Lottery. Lotteries, as the means to raise money for great national projects, are far from new to this country. It was a public lottery that raised the £300,000 necessary for the establishment of the British Museum back in the eighteenth century. In cultural terms, the Lottery represents 'jam today', enabling the creation of new capital projects in an area of public life that has long been starved of funding.

Computer-generated image of Norman Foster's scheme, which includes a glass roof over the Great Court of the British Museum.

The unprecedented success of the Lottery has resulted in nothing less than a complete makeover of some of London's best-known public buildings. Norman Foster's scheme for the expansion of the British Museum comprises a glazed roof over the central Great Court, with the new enclosure providing space for exhibition galleries, an education centre, shops, restaurants and a café. Another big glass roof is a feature of the redevelopment of the National Maritime Museum in Greenwich, the work of American architect (but long-term London resident) Rick Mather, who has also brought his subtle intelligence to bear on the revamping of the Dulwich Picture Gallery, the Wallace Collection and – the greatest challenge of all – the South Bank arts complex. The Science Museum has gained The Wellcome wing, the Imperial War Museum has a new six-storey extension housing the Holocaust Exhibition, and there is a new wing (and rooftop restaurant) for the National Portrait Gallery. On the river Somerset House, designed by Sir William Chambers in the eighteenth century and formerly occupied by the National Records Office and the Inland Revenue, gains a new role as the home of the Gilbert Collection of decorative arts and the Courtauld Institute's department of digital and video art. Its huge car park is now a public piazza/concert venue, complete with fountains and surrounded by shops and places for eating.

Many of these grand projects are clever updates of existing institutions. More conspicuous and potentially much more profound in its influence is Tate Modern at Bankside, whose £50 million Lottery grant (against a total budget of £134 million) was one of the first large awards. The first national museum of modern art in Britain, Tate Modern is the new home of the Tate Gallery's collection of contemporary art; its predecessor has been relaunched (also with the aid of Lottery funds) as Tate Britain.

Sited in a defunct power station, the Bankside museum represents one of the most ambitious conversions of a redundant building that London has ever seen. Bankside Power Station was designed by Sir Giles Gilbert Scott, who was also responsible for another Thames-side landmark, Battersea Power Station, as well as the red London telephone box. Battersea still awaits its fate, but Bankside has been transformed by Swiss architects Herzog & de Meuron into a true cathedral of modern culture. A glazed addition across the top of the severe brick building creates new upper storeys flooded with light, while the stunning central space, the Turbine Hall, derives much of its power from sheer volume – it is 160 metres long and 30 metres high. It took siteworkers two years just to remove the plant and machinery.

The contents of the Millennium Dome in Greenwich have been the source of much criticism since it opened to the public. It nonetheless provides a distinctive and beautiful architectural profile in a very run-down area.

The raw energy of this former industrial building is complemented by a new approach to the display of contemporary art. Rather than arranging work in a sequence or progression, pieces are presented in provocative juxtapositions, making connections between art and life.

The Millennium Dome in Greenwich took yet another approach to display, organising its content, exhibits and activities into 14 human 'zones' such as mind, body, work, play, learning and faith. When in 1997 I was asked to give my thoughts on the direction of the Dome, my recommendation was to get an architect or designer to create an overall vision, much as Hugh Casson did for the Festival of Britain, and Nicholas Serota did in 2000 for Tate Modern. Sadly my advice was ignored.

The degree of funding and creative energy devoted to such large-scale public projects might lead one to suspect that Londoners spend all of their free time on cultural improvement. One might argue that the true vitality of the city, however, springs from the bubbling subculture of its clubs and bars and music venues, a shifting scene that is no sooner identified with a particular place than it has shifted off somewhere else. London boasts a huge range of music venues, from the Wigmore Hall to Ronnie Scott's, from churches such as St Martin-in-the-Fields (where Handel and Mozart both played the organ) to the grassy slopes outside Kenwood House where open-air concerts take place on balmy summer evenings. But it is the pop industry, one of the country's biggest exporters, that is responsible for turning a certain pedestrian crossing in Abbey Road into one of the most popular of all tourist photo opportunities. Like the Rolling Stones on Eel Pie Island, Jimmy Hendrix at the Marquee, the Sex Pistols at World's End and Boy George at the 1980s club Blitz, many London locations, past and present, are inextricably linked with the short but vivid history of rock 'n' roll.

London, in common with most great cities, offers many opportunities for shared experience. Despite the increased commercialization of sport, which has seen corporate logos emblazoned on everything from football shirts to cricket bats, London's sporting fixtures are still a huge draw. Never mind that television coverage provides a better picture of what is happening on the pitch, simply being part of the crowd is irresistible for the seasoned supporter. Certain streets in north London still resemble the *Marie Celeste* when Arsenal are playing at home; Wimbledon fortnight sees fans queuing overnight to secure seats on Centre Court. Crowds still line the towpaths along the Thames to watch the annual Oxford and Cambridge Boat Race,

just as they turn out for that relative newcomer, the London Marathon, or flock to Wembley, Lord's or Twickenham for the big international tournaments that England never quite manages to win. Inevitably, watching athletes compete has a tendency to provoke the less-than-fit to get out of their armchairs. The knock-on effect is such that, during Wimbledon, it is virtually impossible to book a tennis court in London. From health clubs to yoga classes to swimming sessions at the local pool, time out for many Londoners can mean the very serious business of keeping fit.

Less wholesomely, or more colourfully – depending on your point of view – London inevitably offers a range of diversions of the kind that rarely makes an appearance in the pages of a listings magazine. Any metropolis promises the comforting blanket of anonymity for those

Cricket enters the twenty-first century with the futuristic Media Centre, at Lord's Cricket Ground, designed by Future Systems (ABOVE). The Mound Stand, designed by Michael Hopkins, provides a sheltering canopy for spectators (TOP).

Racy sights in Soho.

seeking the pleasures of the flesh, and London is no exception. The sex shops, massage parlours and peepshows of Soho, the tawdry vice market around King's Cross and the odd suburban brothel that makes it into the news are but the visible tip of a very large iceberg indeed. But the truly astonishing aspect of London's sex life is how relatively hidden and inconspicuous it is today in comparison with previous centuries.

The south bank of the Thames, an area originally outside the city's control, had a long association with vice and criminality. From medieval times until the seventeenth century it was a centre of prostitution, with brothels or 'stews' clustered along the river west of London Bridge. This district, known as the Clink, was owned and administered by the Bishop of Winchester. Brothels were virtually licensed premises. They paid rents to the diocese, which, in turn, attempted to regulate the 'oldest profession' by imposing certain (fairly loose) rules of conduct.

From the 1600s onwards the sex trade was increasingly focused on Covent Garden, where many coffee houses and taverns commonly offered rather more than the usual food and drink. An eighteenth-century guide to such illicit pleasures was Harris's *List of Covent Garden Ladies*; Marylebone was also known for its houses of ill repute. In a recent episode of the BBC documentary series *One Foot in the Past* Dan Cruikshank, an expert on Georgian London, revealed the extent to which the sex industry fuelled the development of the city in the eighteenth century. We may pride ourselves on our liberal attitudes, but it seems that the Georgians could teach us a thing or two about broad-mindedness. Sex was a relatively open affair, with brothels as commonplace and as frequently visited as theatres. By the end of the century it was estimated that there were an amazing 25,000 prostitutes in the city, representing one in eight of the adult female population. Many successful courtesans and madams became property developers, contributing to the economic expansion of the period.

Victorian attitudes to sex were, on the surface at least, very different. While the London that Dickens first knew was every bit as licentious as it had been half a century previously, and the sex trade just as visible for anyone who cared to venture into the 'rookeries' or maze-like tenement areas, such activities were increasingly condemned over the succeeding decades. One of the most notorious areas for all types of crime was the rookery of St Giles that extended from Great Russell Street to Long Acre, an area whose inhabitants inspired many of Dickens' most colourful creations. Slum clearance, urban sanitation and other civic improvements brought new light into the city's dark places as the century progressed. Public figures, famously

Gladstone while he was Prime Minister, began to concern themselves with the plight of 'fallen women'; Dickens himself founded a charitable venture that rescued prostitutes from the street and sponsored them to begin new lives in the colonies.

The Victorians would certainly be shocked by some of London's racier sights today and its apparent toleration of different sexual preferences; the Georgians, however, would probably wonder what all the fuss was about. While protection of society's most vulnerable must always remain a priority, the 'sexiness' of a city like London, its sense of risk and allure, is part of what makes it an exciting place – nip into any telephone box for confirmation!

The relative freedom and anonymity of a big city draws outsiders like magnets, and the more diverse the intake, the more varied and potentially exhilarating the social life. In the nature of things, my social life in London seems taken up by a disproportionate number of openings, private views and launch parties – many of which are hugely enjoyable, if at times somewhat exclusive occasions. Exclusive or not, London buzzes with parties, commemorating something or other: weddings and bar mitzvahs, end-of-term degree shows, bonfire parties and barbecues, impromptu after work parties of the thank-goodness-it's-Friday variety. Thursday nights in the City of London are positively Hogarthian, with most of Essex drinking itself silly and just missing the last train home ….

But perhaps the greatest entertainment value of all is provided simply by the spectacle of the street, the animation and vigour of a city of immense contrasts. In the early eighteenth century Samuel Johnson's biographer, James Boswell, was so inspired by this aspect of London as to write: '… the immense crowd and hurry and bustle of business and diversion, the great number of public places of entertainment, the noble churches and superb buildings of different kinds, agitate, amuse, and elevate the mind …. Here a young man of curiosity and observation may have a sufficient fund of present entertainment, and may lay up ideas to employ his mind in age.' It's no different today.

A fishing competition on the banks of Regent's Canal.

OVERLEAF: **A dramatic statement in an artistic installation with figures suspended on the bungee crane at Battersea Power Station (LEFT); skaters at Broadgate ice rink near Liverpool Street Station (RIGHT).**

Europe's largest street festival, the Notting Hill Carnival, originated in the 1960s as a small local event but now attracts over a million tourists, spectators and participants to West London every year (LEFT). For the Sunday and Monday of August Bank Holiday, the streets reverberate in an exuberant celebration of Afro-Caribbean culture.

Late January or early February is the time of the Chinese New Year celebrations, when a noisy, colourful procession winds around the streets of Chinatown, located between Leicester Square and Shaftesbury Avenue (LEFT AND RIGHT). The Chinese population in London is around 60,000 and while few actually live in Chinatown, it remains a popular cultural and community centre.

PREVIOUS PAGES: Cheering the Reds … or the Blues. London football clubs Arsenal

(LEFT) and Chelsea (RIGHT) enjoy the acclaim of their supporters.

Just a perfect day in Soho. Once a smart residential district, Soho became notorious for its bohemian haunts and as the conspicuous home of London's sex trade. Now chic new bars and restaurants have been added to the mix, making this one of the most vibrant areas of the capital and also one that has strong links with the gay community.

The Wallace Collection, based in a late-eighteenth-century house in Manchester Square, has long been one of London's unsung treasures (ABOVE); it has recently benefited from sensitive additions by Rick Mather which include a new café. The Sackler Wing at the Royal Academy of Arts on Piccadilly comprises galleries and a glass atrium designed by Norman Foster (RIGHT).

Sigmund Freud spent the last year of his life in this Hampstead house, after fleeing Nazi persecution in 1938. The house is now a museum; the study and library (featuring the famous couch) remain exactly as they were during Freud's brief tenure (BELOW LEFT). *From the Freud Museum*, Susan Hiller's collection of objects and texts inspired by the Freud Museum is on display at Tate Modern (BELOW).

Eduardo Paolozzi's gigantic statue of Sir Isaac Newton dominates the piazza of the new British Library on the Euston Road, one of the most controversial and heavily criticized public projects ever undertaken in the capital (TOP RIGHT). The building, designed by Colin St John Wilson, was years late and millions over budget when it finally opened in 1998, and its architectural style was somewhat out of fashion. The superb detailing and craftsmanship of the interior, however, have won much praise. At a time when years of cutbacks in local government spending have wreaked havoc on London's public libraries, the opening of a new library is the cause of much celebration. Peckham Library in south London, by Alsop and Stormer, forms part of a scheme to regenerate the heart of this run-down area (CENTRE RIGHT AND BELOW RIGHT). In the heart of St James's, the London Library is a private library founded in 1841 by Thomas Carlyle (LEFT). Members pay an annual subscription for the delicious pleasures of rummaging around in the stacks.

Britain was never supposed to be a very visual culture, but the recent impact of the YBAs (Young British Artists), the arrival of Tate Modern and the programme of museum improvements funded by the Lottery have placed art at the centre of the picture. Small private galleries, such as White Cube 2, a newcomer to Hoxton in east London (ABOVE LEFT), flourish alongside old favourites such as the Tate (ABOVE RIGHT) – newly rechristened Tate Britain. Children enjoy the tactile qualities of Thomas Heatherwick's *Materials House*, a permanent exhibit made of 213 layers of different materials at the Science Museum in South Kensington (RIGHT).

For opera-lovers and balletomanes the controversy about seat prices may still rumble on, but few question the dramatic improvements Jeremy Dixon has achieved in his redesign of the Royal Opera House, Covent Garden. The beautiful red velvet and gilt auditorium, now restored, represents less than a tenth of the entire complex (ABOVE). New access ways link 'The House' with Covent Garden, and the soaring light-filled Floral Hall, rebuilt as a foyer, now serves as an appropriately theatrical curtain-raiser. Behind the scenes, there is equal dedication to the needs of performers. For the first time, dancers of the Royal Ballet have on-site rehearsal studios (ABOVE RIGHT).

OVERLEAF: **Children's adventure playground in Wapping, east London (LEFT); Centre Court at Wimbledon, home of the Lawn Tennis Championships (RIGHT).**

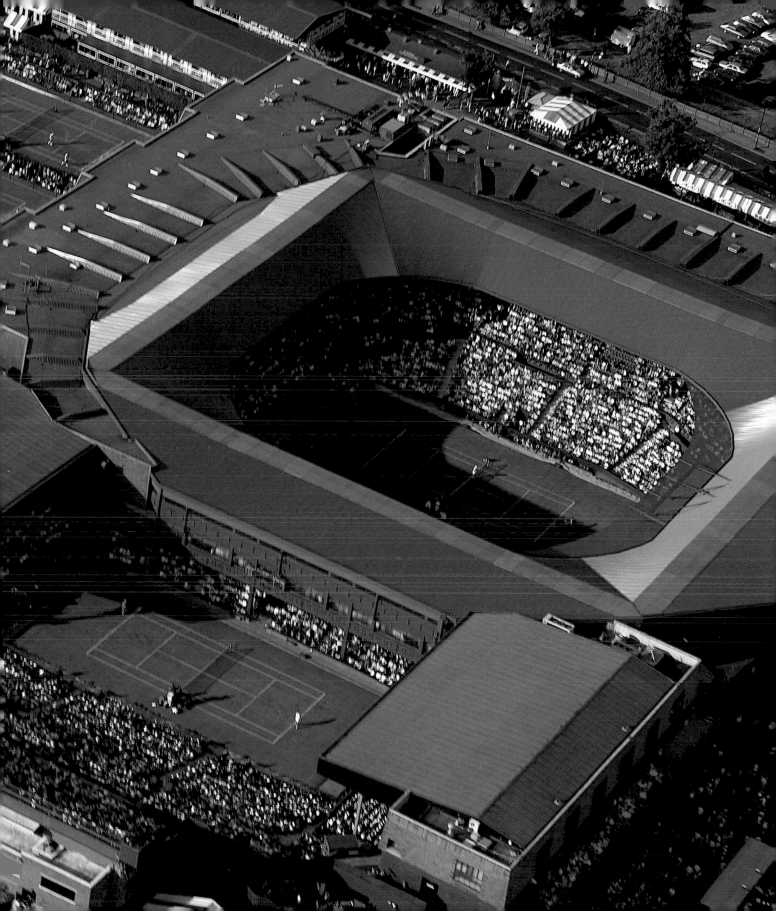

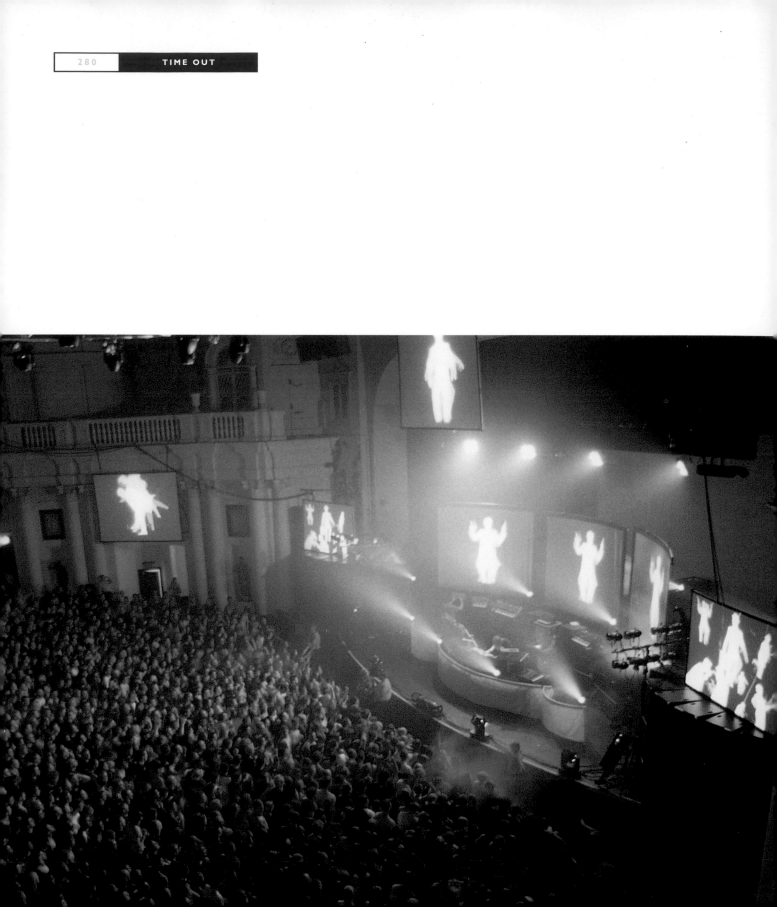

In an age of passive, electronic entertainment, live performance provides an invaluable sense of immediacy and participation. London boasts hundreds of music venues, from tiny clubs and intimate jazz bars to halls such as the Brixton Academy, here the venue for a sell-out show by the Chemical Brothers (LEFT). The Royal Court in Sloane Square has an impressive history as one of the leading theatres for contemporary British drama (ABOVE). The building was dangerously unsafe when architects Haworth Tomkins undertook a programme of renovation. Their refurbishment carefully integrated new services and facilities while preserving the delicate sense of theatrical community.

London's surviving grand old picture palaces include the Art Deco cinema in Kilburn (ABOVE) and the Phoenix in Finchley (BELOW, FAR RIGHT). After a recent revamp, the Rio in Dalston continues to serve the local community with mainstream and arthouse films (CENTRE). The new BFI London IMAX cinema at Waterloo shows 3D features (TOP); the Lux in Hoxton is a new repertory cinema that also serves as a centre for experimental film-makers (TOP RIGHT).

Pleasures of the flesh: the titillating window of **Agent Provocateur**, the **Soho** shop specializing in sexy underwear (LEFT); participants in the annual **Gay Pride** march (TOP); postcards in telephone kiosks advertise the oldest profession (ABOVE).

A walk on the wild side at Madame JoJo's, a transvestite club in Soho.

A bewildering variety of commercial enterprises operate 'underneath the arches' in the cheap premises below elevated sections of railway line. In the City, Cannons Health Club provides a memorable place for a swim (ABOVE LEFT). Berthold Lubetkin's Penguin Pool at London Zoo, designed by the Russian emigré in the 1930s, is a modernist masterpiece (ABOVE). The penguins, however, feel rather differently about it. Lubetkin sited nesting boxes a little too close together for comfort and delicate negotiations are now under way between zookeepers and architectural heritage experts to make the pool more penguin-friendly without compromising the beauty of the design.

A spectacular laser and light show marked the launch of Tate Modern (ABOVE). Swiss architects Herzog & de Meuron have maintained the raw energy of the vast Turbine Hall (RIGHT), adding a 'light box' of galleries across the top of the building.

Favourite Haunts

Here is a selection of interesting spots to visit in London, many of them located a little off the beaten track. London boasts a multitude of hidden attractions – places that can be fun, quirky, secluded, mysterious, romantic or sexy – and they are all there waiting to be unearthed. Perhaps this selection will tempt you to make your own discoveries or to revisit places that you have not explored for years.

London at Home

Fenton House, Windmill Hill NW3 (020 7435 3471)

A seventeenth-century house open throughout the summer, home to an outstanding collection of porcelain and early keyboard instruments, and blessed with a superb walled garden.

Fournier Street E1

A row of eighteenth-century houses where the silk-weaving French Huguenot community once lived.

2 Willow Road NW3 (020 7435 6166)

A modernist terrace house built for himself by Ernö Goldfinger in the 1930s and now run by the National Trust.

Isokon Flats, Well Road NW3

Fantastic 1930s architecture; Walter Gropius used to live here.

Savile Row Police Station W1 (020 7321 8706)

If you happen to get arrested in London, this is probably the best place to spend the night.

Dennis Severs House, 18 Folgate Street E1 (020 7247 4013)

On the first Sunday of each month you can savour a wonderful theatrical experience here, wandering around recreated eighteenth- and nineteenth-century interiors put together by the late Dennis Severs, a designer and performer.

Trinity Church Square SE1

A beautiful residential square close to Elephant and Castle.

Transport

Greenwich Foot Tunnel SE10–E14

Running between Greenwich Pier and Island Gardens in the Isle of Dogs, this passageway beneath the Thames is 370 metres long and lined with more than 200,000 tiles.

Jubilee Line Stations (020 7308 2800)

Sample the distinctive and impressive character of the new stations on the Jubilee Line, from Southwark to North Greenwich.

Millennium Footbridge SE1–EC1

Not initially the best way of crossing the river between St Paul's and Tate Modern, given its closure for adjustments soon after opening, but it imparts new architectural interest to this developing part of Bankside.

St Pancras Station, Euston Road NW1 (020 7918 1704)

One of the finest examples of Victorian station architecture.

Thames Barrier, Unity Way SE18

Best seen by boat, the barrier's gates stretch 520 metres across the river.

Work

Hatton Garden EC1

London's diamond and jewellery district.

The Inns of Court, Holborn W1

The four surviving Inns of Court (Gray's Inn: 020 7458 7800, Lincoln's Inn: 020 7405 1394, Inner Temple: 020 7797 8250 and Middle Temple: 020 7429 4800) constitute the heart of the English legal system. Barristers are required to study at one of the Inns and 'eat dinners' before the Inns can call them to the Bar. Lincoln's Inn dates right back to the fifteenth century.

Lloyd's Building, 1 Lime Street EC3 (020 7327 1000)

Richard Rogers' extraordinary 1984 architectural creation, with exposed stainless-steel ductwork and lift shaft.

Royal Geographical Society, 1 Kensington Gore SW7 (020 7591 3000)

The Society is based in Lowther Lodge, designed by Norman Shaw. The map room is open to the public (for a £10 fee).

100% Design, Earl's Court, Warwick Road SW5 (020 7385 1200)

This annual contemporary design show has become an essential fixture on the design calendar; it usually takes place each autumn.

Shopping

Alfie's Antique Market, 13 Church Street NW8 (020 7723 6066)

A rabbit warren of a flea market, comprising permanent shops and stalls selling antique and vintage collectibles.

Bermondsey Market, Bermondsey Square SE1

A treasure trove of antique furniture for traders and bargain hunters alike. Get there early. Every Friday, 5am to 2pm.

Columbia Road Market, Columbia Road E2

A Sunday-morning market for flowers, shrubs and bedding plants, also offering great street food and surrounded by inviting shops and cafés.

Cyberdog, 9 Earlham Street WC2 (020 7836 7855)

Clothes and accessories for the dedicated clubber, with futuristic sculptures and insanely loud banging techno music.

Mr Eddie, Berwick Street W1 (020 7437 3727)

This tailor makes bespoke velvet suits.

Gabriel's Wharf SE1

An eclectic collection of shops, restaurants and bars located on the South Bank. A tiny bandstand is the venue for live music throughout the summer.

The Pineal Eye, 49 Broadwick Street W1 (020 7434 2567)
Stockists of the weird and wonderful, from fur nails to hair-sprouting beauty spots.

Stanford's, 12–14 Long Acre WC2 (020 7836 1321)
A specialist retailer of a huge and comprehensive selection of maps of virtually anywhere in the world.

Eating and Drinking

The Bagel Bake, Brick Lane E1
An East London institution, open 24 hours a day. Bagels are baked on the premises.

Café Cairo, Landor Road SW9 (020 7771 1201)
A café on an Egyptian theme, set up and run by a former BBC travel journalist. Full of bongs, Bedouin tents, whips and pouffes, it has a wonderfully exotic, smoky, late-night atmosphere.

Gordon's Wine Bar, 47 Villiers Street WC2 (020 7930 1408)
In vaulted cellars deep beneath the street, this dark and cavernous bar boasts a great wine list.

Graceland Palace, 881 Old Kent Road SE1 (020 7639 3961)
Sample superb Chinese food as an Elvis impersonator sings his heart out.

The Griffin, 125 Clerkenwell Road EC1 (020 7405 3855)
At first glance this pub looks like your average local boozer. And it is, but there are table dancers in one corner; pop your pound in their pint glass, and enjoy the show!

The Market Porter, 9 Stoney Street SE1
Next to Borough market and open at 6am for an early morning tipple.

Patisserie Valerie, 44 Old Compton Street W1 (020 7437 3466)
An authentic French café, beloved of art students, serving delicious cream cakes, fruit tarts and coffee.

The Red Lion, 23 Crown Passage SW1 (020 7930 4141)
A small old local pub in the heart of clubland. The door to the gents' toilets is so small that you might not make it through after a few too many.

Shanghai Chinese Restaurant, 41 Kingsland High Street E8 (020 7254 2878)
Located in a listed building, this was formerly an eel, pie and mash shop. Worth visiting to see the original tiled interior.

Green London

Brockwell Park Lido, Dulwich Road SE24 (020 7274 3088)
A stunning location for open-air swimming. Hardly a secret on a summer weekend, but far less crowded during the week.

Buddhist Peace Pagoda, Battersea Park SW11
Erected by Japanese Buddhists in 1985, the pagoda features four large gilded Buddhas.

Camden to Little Venice Canal Walk NW1–W2
London's waterways stretch for miles but this section is particularly picturesque, especially early in the morning.

Chelsea Physic Garden, 66 Royal Hospital Road SW3 (020 7352 5646)
Established in 1673 to study plants for medicinal use.

Hampstead Heath NW3
Some 800 acres of green space with 28 natural ponds. Three of the ponds are used for swimming; there is one for men, one for women and one for mixed bathing.

Highgate Cemetery, Swain's Lane N6 (020 8340 1834)
Karl Marx's grave is in the East Cemetery. The Gothic splendour of the West Cemetery was the inspiration for *Dracula*.

Hill Garden, Golder's Hill, Hampstead Heath NW3

This formal garden, with its pretty pond and walkway sheltered by a pergola, is one of the hidden treasures of the Heath.

Mount Street Gardens W1

Small private gardens with a hidden entrance behind the flowerseller opposite Harry's Bar. Go in April, sit on the benches dedicated to lost lovers, and admire the carpet of fallen pink and white blossom.

Regent's Park Open-Air Theatre, Regent's Park NW1 (020 7486 2431)

Venue for open-air performances of Shakespeare, opera and ballet throughout the summer.

Speakers' Corner, Marble Arch, Hyde Park W1

Perfect for Sunday-morning heckling, as one-member political parties stand on their soapboxes and tell us how they will make the world a better place.

Vauxhall City Farm, Tyers Street SE11 (020 7582 4204)

One of 20 city farms scattered throughout the capital. A great place for introducing children to sheep, goats, ferrets, chickens and numerous other small animals.

Time Out

Barbican Centre, Silk Street EC2 (020 7638 8891)

The conservatory above the Barbican arts centre is a surprising oasis in the middle of the concrete-dominated city.

Bethnal Green Museum of Childhood, Cambridge Heath Road E2 (020 8980 2415)

A superb collection of toys and dolls' houses can be enjoyed in this purpose-built branch of the V&A Museum.

Broadgate Ice Rink, Broadgate Circle EC2 (020 7505 4068)

Open-air ice skating in winter in the heart of the City.

Brompton Oratory, Brompton Road SW1 (020 7808 0900)

A Roman Catholic church with a sumptuous baroque interior, dating from the late nineteenth century.

Circus Space, Coronet Street N1 (020 7613 4141)

Training and degree courses for would-be acrobats, trapeze artists and other performers are on offer at the former Shoreditch Power Station.

Dulwich Picture Gallery, College Road SE21 (020 8693 5254)

The oldest public art gallery in England houses a splendid collection including works by Rembrandt, Raphael and Canaletto.

The Fencing Club, Natural History Museum, Cromwell Road SW7 (020 7942 5736)

A small and informal club whose members keep the emphasis on the fun of the sport.

Fountain Court, Somerset House, The Strand WC2 (020 7848 2526)

Hidden from The Strand, this beautiful courtyard features a show of dancing water and light.

Greek Orthodox Cathedral of St Sophia, Moscow Road W2 (020 7229 7260)

The focus of the local Greek community, the cathedral boasts a richly decorated interior with a compelling display of icons.

The Halloween Society, 206 Panther House, 38 Mount Pleasant WC1 (020 7833 1009)

This roving cinema shows short, quirky films in a variety of venues. You can take your own drinks, sit at the tables and, should you so wish, smoke to your heart's content.

Hawksmoor's churches:
St Mary Woolnoth, Lombard Street EC3 (020 7626 9701);
St George's Bloomsbury, Bloomsbury Way WC1 (020 7405 3044);
St George-in-the-East, Cannon Street Road E1 (020 7481 1345);
Christ Church, Commercial Street E1 (020 7247 7202)
These churches display the awe-inspiring baroque architecture of Wren's most talented pupil, Nicholas Hawksmoor. Christ Church is an especially impressive example.

The House of 10,000 Secrets, 12 Stephenson Way NW1 (020 7387 2222)
The home of the Magic Circle, and an Aladdin's Cave of magic paraphernalia.

Sir John Soane's Museum, Lincoln's Inn Fields WC2 (020 7405 2107)
One of London's most idiosyncratic museums, housing the curios and antiquities collected by Sir John Soane, the leading neo-classical architect.

The Lux Cinema, 2–4 Hoxton Square N1 (020 7684 0200)
A comfortable cinema that shows a fine selection of repertory films.

Monument EC3
A 62-metre-high monument to the Great Fire of London, designed by Sir Christopher Wren and standing near the spot where the fire started in Pudding Lane.

Oasis Swimming Pool, 32 Endell Street WC2 (020 7831 1804)
Swim in the open air in the centre of town.

Old Operating Theatre Museum and Herb Garret, 9a St Thomas Street SE1 (020 7955 4791)
This is fitted out just as it was in the nineteenth century, with sawdust on the floor to soak up the blood!

Poets' Corner, Westminster Abbey, Parliament Square SW1 (020 7222 5152)
Memorials to Chaucer, Shakespeare, Milton, Dickens and numerous literary greats.

St Stephen Walbrook, Walbrook EC4 (020 7283 4444)
A massive white stone altar by Sir Henry Moore stands in this Sir Christopher Wren church. There is also a monument to Rector Chad Varah who founded The Samaritans in 1953.

Walthamstow Stadium, Chingford Mount Road E4 (020 8498 3300)
London's most prestigious dog-racing track.

Wimbledon Stadium, Plough Lane SW17 (020 8946 8000)
There is regular greyhound racing here, and on every other Sunday an amazingly destructive evening of banger racing.

York Hall Turkish Bath, Bethnal Green Road E1 (020 8980 2243)
There are few better ways to relax after a hard day at the office than to visit this remarkable Turkish bath for a steam and sauna.

Index

Acknowledgements

Author's acknowledgements

I would like to thank the whole team who made this book such a pleasure to work on. The most difficult thing was cutting it down to size, as there was so much we wanted to say and show, but sadly it had to fit inside the M25. In particular, my thanks to Liz Wilhide and Steven Blackman who charmingly cajoled and prodded me to examine recessive corners of my memory and when they were empty filled them with their own ideas. And welcome to our new Mayor. London needs him.

Special photography

Louise Service would like to thank the following people for their help with the special photography features: staff and customers at Billingsgate Fish Market; the staff at Clapton Garage and those on the 38 Route; the staff at Madame JoJo's; and all those at the Great Eastern hotel, especially Victoria and Simon. Many thanks also to Helen Lewis for commissioning the photographs.

The Publisher would like to thank Sarah Hopper for her assistance with picture research. The Publisher also thanks the following photographers and organisations for their permission to reproduce the photographs in this book:

Endpapers NERC/Earth Images; 2–3 Alan Williams/Axiom; 4–5 Mary Winch/Axiom; 6 Alberto Arzoz/Axiom; 7 Antonio Olmos; 9 Jonathan Glynn-Smith/Celebrity Pictures; 12 Richard McCaig/Impact; 14 &15 Richard Bryant/Arcaid(Architects: Stirling & Wilford);16 Travel pix/The Telegraph Colour Library;18 above left Alan Keohane/Impact;18 above right Simon Shepheard/Impact;18 below left Alexis Wallerstein/Impact;18 below right Brian Boyd/Colorific Photo Library Ltd;19 above left Ian Bell/London Transport HQ;19 above right Julian Anderson;19 below left Christian Sarramon;19 below right Antonio Olmos; 21 Ben Edwards/Impact; 22 above David Harden/Impact; 22 below Petteri Kokkonen/Impact; 24 Mohamed Ansar/Impact; 25 Lewis/Edifice; 27 Skyscan Photo Library; 30 left John Hammond/By permission of the trustees of Dulwich Picture Gallery(Rick Mather Architects); 30–31 Dennis Gilbert/View(Architects: Jeremy Dixon/Edward Jones); 31 right Richard Bryant/Arcaid(Design: Iskipp & Jenkins); 33 above left & right Skyscan Photo Library; 33 below David Norton/Telegraph Colour Library; 34 & 35 James Morris/Axiom; 36–37 Ian Lambot/Arcaid; 38 Graham Trott; 40 Antonio Olmos; 41 Rex Features; 42 Worpole/Edifice; 43 Marcus Harpur; 44 Mike McQueen/Impact; 45 & 47 David Hoffman Photo Library; 48–49 Graham Trott; 50 above Antonio Olmos; 50 below Phillip Simpson; 51 Alberto Arzoz/Axiom; 52 above Arcaid(Owner: Robin & Lucienne Day); 52 below Tim MacPherson; 53 above Dennis Gilbert/National Trust Photo Library(Owner: Goldfinger); 53 below Philip Harris/National Trust Photo Library(Owner: Goldfinger); 54 above left Martin Jones/Arcaid; 54 above right Today/Rex Features; 54 below left Bill Burlington/Arcaid; 54 below right Phillip Simpson; 55 Nigel Spalding; 56 Clive Frost; 57 Ray Main/Mainstream; 58 left Anthony Oliver(Owner: Karen Savage); 58 above right Anthony Oliver; 58 below right Clive Frost(Owner: Jamie Cahn); 59 Tim MacPherson;60 Nigel Spalding; 61 Mark Fiennes/Arcaid; 62 Ray Main/Mainstream(Architect: Andrew Martin); 63 Ray Main/Mainstream; 64 Steve Pyke; 65 Simon Upton/World of Interiors May 2000; 66 Ken Kirkwood/In English Style by Suzanne Slesin & Stafford Cliff; 67 Universal Pictorial Press; 68 left Robert O' Dea/Arcaid;68 above, centre, below right Bill Burlington/Arcaid; 69 Jason Bell/Evening Standard Magazine; 70 left & main picture Richard Bryant/Arcaid(Architect: Richard Rogers); 71 Peter Cook/View(Architect: Fiona McLean); 73 Max Jourdan/Camera Press; 74 left Alberto Arzoz/Axiom; 74 above, centre & below right Artist: Ron Hazeldon, in association with Robert Ian Barnes Architects; 75 above, centre and below courtesy of Maggie Elenby; 76 Tom McGhee/The Image Bank; 77 Gari Wyn Williams/Colorific Photo Library Ltd; 78 Dave Young; 80 Ian Bell/London Transport HQ; 81 Tate Gallery Publications,(Artist: Simon Patterson); 83 Post Office Communications; 84 Brian E.Rybolt/Impact; 86 Dennis Gilbert/View(Architects: Foster Associates); 87 Thames Water Picture Library; 88 Antonio Olmos; 89 Ray Main/Mainstream; 90–91 Max Jourdan/Camera Press; 92 Rod Morris; 93 Alexis Wallerstein/Impact; 94–95 courtesy of Evening Standard; 95 Daily Express; 96 The Stock Market; 97 PA News;100–101 Al Chandler/courtesy of The Automobile Association;102 above Clive Frost;102 Dennis Gilbert(Architects: Foster Associates); 103 above left Dennis Gilbert/View(Architects: MacCormac Jamieson Pritchard); 103 above right Dennis Gilbert/View(Architect: Alsop, Lyall & Stormer); 103 below Dennis Gilbert/View(Weston Williams Architects); 104 Peter Cook/View(Architects: Nicholas Grimshaw & Partners);105 Nick Hufton/View (Architects: Nicholas Grimshaw & Partners); 106 Johnathan Player/Rex Features; 107 Dave Young; 108 Dod Miller/Network; 110 David Levenson/Colorific Photo Library

Ltd; 111 Debbie Treloar/Conran Octopus; 113 University of East London; 114 Paul Avis; 115 above & below PA News(Designer: Hussein Chalayan); 117 Paul Stuart/BBC; 118–119 Eddie Ryle-Hodges/Edifice; 119 Michael Freeman/Telegraph Colour Library; 120 Mark Henley/Impact; 121 Richard Turpin/Arcaid; 122 Steve Benbow/Colorific Photo Library Ltd; 122 above Christophe Bluntzer/Impact; 122 below & 123 Simon Shepheard/Impact; 124 Homer Sykes/Impact; 125 above Gary Calton/Camera Press; 125 below Antonio Olmos; 126 &127 Anthony Oliver; 128 Tony Page/Impact; 129 Rupert Conant/Impact; 130 Stephen Gill;131 Richard Bryant/Arcaid(Architect: Foster Associates); 134 Sean Smith/The Guardian; 136 R. Stonehouse/Camera Press; 137 Julian Anderson(Designer: Alexander McQueen); 138 & 139 Luke White (commissioned by Evening Standard Magazine); 140 above left Mark Henley/Impact; 140 above right Theodore Wood/Camera Press; 140 below Paul Reas/Network; 141 Rex Features; 142 Amelia Troubridge/Truman Brewery; 143 right Clive Frost; 144–145 James Morris/Axiom(Architect: Foster Associates); 146 Mario Testino/courtesy of Paul Smith; 147 courtesy of Fortnum & Mason+; 148 courtesy of The Hive; 149 Steve Speller/Design:Thomas Heatherwick Studio; 150 Georgia Glynn-Smith/courtesy of The Conran Shop; 151 Gary Calton/Camera Press; 152 Edina van der Wyck/The Interior Archive; 153 Georgia Glynn Smith/courtesy of Conran Restaurants(Designer: Terence Conran); 156–157 Morley Von Sternberg/courtesy of Erica Bolton & Jane Quinn(Artist: Sam Taylor-Wood); 158 courtesy of Jesse James; 158 above left courtesy of Timothy Glazier Associates; 158 above right Paul Avis/Conran Octopus; 158 below left Wayne Vincent/The Interior Archive; 159 above Martin Jones/Arcaid; 159 above Christopher Simon-Sykes/The Interior Archive; 159 centre Christian Sarramon; 159 centre right Josh Pullman/phPR (courtesy of Angela Hale); 159 below courtesy of Pickett Leather; 159 below left Paul Avis/Conran Octopus; 160 Gary Calton/Camera Press; 161 Paul Avis; 162 above Chrisophe Bluntzer/Impact; 162 below Julian Anderson; 163 Cedric Arnold/Truman Brewery; 163 below Steven Tilley/Truman Brewery; 164–165 above Richard Glover(Architect: John Pawson); 165 below Chris Doyle; 166 Simon Upton/The Interior Archive(Owner: Lulu Guiness); 167 Clive Frost(designer: Alexander McQueen); 168 left Ben Smith/courtesy of Flowercity(Designer: Laurence J. Lewis); 168 right Chris Gasgoigne/View; 169 Daffyd Jones; 170 Julian Anderson; 171 left Alberto Arzoz/Axiom; 171 right Antonio Olmos; 172 left courtesy of Egg; 173 Chris Doyle; 173 right Dennis Gilbert/View(Architects: McDaniel Wolff); 174 left Conrad Tracey; 174 above right Xavier Cervera/Millennium; 174 below right Paul Lowe/Network; 175 Stephen Gill;176 left Brett Wolstoncroft/courtesy of Daunts Bookstore;177 Them; 177 main picture Christian Sarramon; 178–179 Boris Baggs; 182 Simon Upton/The Interior Archive; 186 Viki Couchman; 187 Martin Brigdale/Anthony Blake Library; 188 Martin Charles(Architects: Long & Kentish); 189 Simon Upton/The Interior Archive; 190 Sean Cunningham/Camera Press; 191 Peter Cook/View(Architects: Manser & Associates/Conran & Partners); 192–193 Gideon Mendel/Network; 194 Nutopia(James Winspear); 195 Xavier Cervera/Millennium; 196 Pascal Latra/The Colony Rooms; 197 John Freeman; 198 Steve Orino; 199 &

200 above Gideon Mendel/Network; 200 below Anthony Oliver; 201 above & below Alberto Arzoz/Axiom; 202–203 Tim Macpherson/Anthony Blake Library; 204 above Chris Gasgoigne/View; 204 below Clive Frost; 205 Phil Starling; 206–207 Tim Macpherson/Anthony Blake Library; 210 Simon Upton/The Interior Archive; 211 Richard Open/Camera Press; 212 Ray Main/Mainstream; 213 Rolant Dafis/Arcaid; 214 The Travel Library; 215 Jerry Harpur; 216 Gettyone Stone; 218 Jerry Harpur; 219 Rolant Dafis; 221 Julian Anderson; 222–223 Bruce Stephens/Impact; 224 Darley/Edifice; 225 Tim MacPherson; 226 David Spero; 227 Phillip Simpson; 228 Andrew Lawson(Designer: Dan Pearson); 229 right Jerry Harpur(Owner: Henrietta Parson); 230 Chrisophe Bluntzer/Impact; 231 David Fillitoe/The Guardian; 231 below Jon Hoffman/Impact; 232–233 Nicola Browne; 234 Alessandro Capodaro/World of Interiors November 1998; 235 Chris Doyle; 236 left Rex Features; 236 right James Morris/Axiom; 237 Simon Shepheard/Impact; 238–239 Gettyone Stone; 240 Andrew Lawson(Designer: Anouska Hemple); 241 Georgia Glynn-Smith(Designer: Arabella Lennox-Boyd) Ltd; 242 Jerry Young(Artist: Bill Woodrow); 243 Nicola Browne; 244 Richard Turpin/Arcaid; 245 Patrick Ward/Colorific Photo Library Ltd; 246–247 Stephen Studd/Gettyone Stone; 248 Keith Hallam/Skyscan Photo Library; 249 Quick UK Ltd/Skyscan Photo Library; 250 Dennis Gilbert/View; 251 Peter Durant/arcblue (Sir Hubert Bennet & Jack Whittle); 252 Rex Features(Actors: Nicole Kidman & Ian Glen); 253 Richard Bryant/Arcaid; 254 courtesy of The Design Museum; 255 British Museum(Architects: Foster & Partners); 256 C. Bowman/Robert Harding; 257 above Lewis/Edifice(Architects: Hopkins Associates/Future Systems); 257 below Lewis/Edifice(Architects: Future Systems); 258 Helen Drew; 259 Peter Arkell/Impact; 260 Clive Shirley/Impact; 261 Adam Woolfit/Robert Harding; 264 Rex Features; 265 Ross Kinnaird/Allsport; 268 Richard Bryant/Arcaid; 269 Royal Academy of Arts; 270 Simon Upton/The Interior Archive; 271 main picture Tate Gallery Publications(Artist: Susan Hiller); 272 Chrisopher Simon Sykes/World of Interiors May 1991; 273 above PA News; 273 centre & below Richard Waite; 274 left Graham Turner/The Guardian; 274 right Mark Henley/Impact; 275 Steve Speller/Design:Thomas Heatherwick Studio, Engineering: Packman Lucas Construction: Make Ltd; 276 Dennis Gilbert/View (Architects: BDP, Dixon Jones); 277 Dennis Gilbert/View(Architects: BDP, Dixon Jones); 278 Skyscan Photo Library; 279 Jason Hawkes/Julian Cotton Photo Library; 280 Amanda Rose/Brixton Academy; 281 David Spero; 282 above left R.Holttom/IMAX cinema; 282 below left Nigel Corrie/English Heritage Photographic Library; 282–283& 283 above Dennis Gilbert/View(Architects: Burrell, Foley, Fischer); 251 below Nigel Corrie/English Heritage Photographic Library; 284 Julian Anderson; 285 above right Tom Webster/Impact; 285 below right Alexis Wallerstein/Impact; 288 Dave Young; 289 James Morris/Axiom; 290 Alberto Arzoz/Axiom; 291 PA News; 304 National Geographic Society Image/Topical Press Agency

Every effort has been made to trace the copyright holders, architects and designers and we apologise in advance for any unintentional omissions, and would be pleased to insert the appropriate acknowledgement in any subsequent publication.

Ladies picnic on the roof of Adelaide House, 1932. Tower Bridge can be seen in the background.

The roof garden incorporated an 18-hole putting green.

First published in 2000 by
Conran Octopus Limited
A part of Octopus Publishing Group
2–4 Heron Quays, London E14 4JP
www.conran-octopus.co.uk

ISBN 1 84901 039 9
Text copyright © Terence Conran 2000
Design and layout copyright © Conran Octopus
2000
Special photography copyright © Louise Service

Managing Director: Caroline Proud
Creative Director: Leslie Harrington

Managing editor: Emma Clegg
Assistant editor: Lucy Nicholson
Editorial assistant: Lara McCann
Copy editor: Libby Willis
Proofreader: Barbara Roby
Indexer: Hilary Bird

Design: Helen Lewis
Picture research: Marissa Keating and
Rachel Davies
Production: Zoe Fawcett and Manjit Sihra

Consultant editor: Liz Wilhide
Special photography: Louise Service

British Library Cataloguing-in-Publication Data.
A catalogue record for this book is available from
the British Library.

Printed in Italy by G. Canale & C. S.p.A.